THE *Life*
GOD BLESSES

Books by Jim Cymbala

Fresh Wind, Fresh Fire
Fresh Faith
Fresh Power
The Life God Blesses

THE *Life* GOD BLESSES

The Secret of Enjoying God's Favor

JIM CYMBALA

PASTOR OF THE BROOKLYN TABERNACLE

with Stephen Sorenson

GRAND RAPIDS, MICHIGAN 49530

ZONDERVAN™

The Life God Blesses
Copyright © 2001 by Jim Cymbala

Requests for information should be addressed to:
Zondervan, *Grand Rapids, Michigan 49530*

   ISBN: 0-310-24202-9

This edition printed on acid-free paper.

Published in association with the literary agency of Ann Spangler & Associates, 1420 Pontiac Road SE, Grand Rapids, MI 49506.

Interior design by Melissa Elenbaas
Printed in the United States of America

01 02 03 04 05 06 07 08 /❖ WZ/ 10 9 8 7 6 5 4 3 2

CONTENTS

PROLOGUE

THE SEARCH

Throughout history mankind has been searching for one thing or another: for knowledge, for new lands, for freedom from religious and political persecution, and for valuable resources such as gold, diamonds, and oil. People have searched for new pleasures, the perfect mate, and peace in the midst of fighting and carnage. There has also been an age-old quest for inner peace and for understanding the real reason for our existence.

Out of this quest comes one of the greatest searches: the one to know and experience God. Inside the human heart is an undeniable, spiritual instinct to commune with its Creator. We can deny, ignore, or bury that instinct under an avalanche of material things, but the fact that we were created to enjoy God and to worship him forever is etched upon our souls.

Countless people have chronicled their search for the Almighty. Testimonies abound of the life-changing nature of an encounter with God, who sent his Son into the world so that men and women "may have life, and have it to the full" (John 10:10). But as interesting as man's quest for God is, it merely points to a far more significant search that I want us to consider in this book.

That search was revealed long ago when God sent a prophet to deliver a message to King Asa in Jerusalem. Although the Lord was correcting Asa for his lack of faith and devotion, the prophetic word contained a declaration that God himself was involved in a unique search! In describing God's love and desire to bless his people, the prophet declared a truth that is staggering in its implications: "For the eyes of the LORD move to and fro throughout the earth that He may strongly support those whose heart is completely

His" (2 Chronicles 16:9 NASB). Since God is unchanging, what was true during King Asa's day applies to us in the twenty-first century.

God is on a search. He is not looking for such things as knowledge or precious stones—after all, he knows everything and owns the world and everything in it. Although we rarely think about this or hear it preached, the Creator of all things is looking throughout the whole earth for a certain kind of heart. He is searching for a human heart that will allow him to show how marvelously he can strengthen, help, and bless someone's life.

Notice that God isn't seeking someone with a high IQ or multiple talents. Nor is he seeking the clever speaker or the person of influence. He revealed where his true interest lies when he sent the prophet Samuel to anoint the future king of Israel. God said, "Do not consider his appearance or his height. . . . The LORD does not look at the things man looks at. Man looks at the outward appearance, but the LORD *looks at the heart*" (1 Samuel 16:7).

What made David special was his heart, and that principle has never changed. All the great men and women of Scripture had *great hearts* that permitted God's grace to flow through them and bring blessings to others. This truth was well understood by David, the young man whom God elevated to the throne. Before he died, David charged his son Solomon, "And you, my son Solomon, acknowledge the God of your father, and serve him with *wholehearted* devotion and with a willing mind, for *the LORD searches every heart* and understands every motive behind the thoughts" (1 Chronicles 28:9). It is what God sees behind the façade and outward behavior that determines the extent of his blessing. So King David wanted his son to pay very careful attention to his heart.

In the New Testament we read how Jesus saw through the outward shows of religion and affirmed the importance of a "right" heart when he condemned the hypocrisy of the Pharisees: "You are the ones who justify yourselves in the eyes of men, but *God knows your hearts*" (Luke 16:15). Jesus always looked into the heart, and there he found the real person.

Christianity is by necessity a religion of the heart because only out of the heart comes "the wellspring of life" (Proverbs 4:23). God calls people to turn to him with their *whole hearts*. Salvation is received when we believe *in our hearts* that God raised Jesus from the dead (Romans 10:9). When Scripture bids us to pray, it asks us to *pour out our hearts* to the Lord (Psalm 62:8). Modern preaching puts an overwhelming emphasis on works and external forms of worship, but a real spiritual revival must always begin in the heart.

Notice the kind of heart to which God is drawn, as seen in Samuel's words to King Saul: "The LORD has sought out a man *after his own heart* and appointed him leader of his people" (1 Samuel 13:14). God's search for a king ended when he found obscure David and his very special heart. But what does it mean to have a special heart, "a heart after God"?

This is a most important subject for us to consider because it speaks to who we really are and to what extent God can use us for his glory. A heart out of tune, out of sync with God's heart, will produce a life of spiritual barrenness and missed opportunities. But as we ask the Lord to bring our hearts into harmony with and submission to his, we will find the secret of his blessings that has remained the same throughout all generations.

ONE

THE MAN WHO WOULDN'T LISTEN

A Sunday night service I will never forget started an unusual series of events I never could have imagined.

We were prepared to serve Communion to the congregation, and I was looking forward to preaching from the Word of God. In addition, a young couple—gospel singers from Nashville— were prepared to sing for us that night. But none of that ever happened. While we were singing praise songs to the Lord, an extended time of free-flowing worship began. As people poured out their adoration to God, an awesome sense of his presence filled the auditorium. All of us were overwhelmed as rivers of deeper and deeper praise ascended from our hearts to the Lord. All sense of time seemed to disappear as we became lost in God's presence. Nothing seemed to matter except worshiping "the Lamb at the center of the throne" (Revelation 7:17), the One who is worthy to be praised forever. It seemed as if wave after wave of God's glory rolled over us as we stood, sat, and knelt before him.

As I looked out over the congregation from the platform, I realized that God was doing a special work among us by his Spirit. A kind of divine surgery was going on as worship and praise mingled with petitions and intercessions. Conviction of sin was very strong, which always happens when the Spirit of God manifests his holy presence among his people. To stop or hinder what was going on seemed like a terrible grieving of the Spirit, so I never even took an offering that evening. The bills would wait. I just could not interrupt the wonderful ways in which the Lord was working in people's lives. The service ended hours later, and people were still kneeling or sitting quietly before the Lord when I finally left the auditorium.

Carol and I arrived home late. We were physically exhausted from a long day of ministering, but our hearts still basked in the afterglow of our time with the Lord. When I came out of the bathroom, Carol was already in bed and had turned on the television. We often watched the national broadcast of one of America's foremost televangelists late on Sunday nights. The program was usually a tape of one of his crusade meetings, and that night was no exception. The televangelist was already preaching his sermon when I began watching from the bathroom doorway.

During the previous months, we had been saddened by the increasingly shrill and harsh spirit of this man's preaching. Instead of carefully and humbly handling God's Word, his preaching was dominated by bombast and denunciations of sinners high and low. But we were not prepared for what he said that night.

As he discussed social evils contaminating America, he referred to a recent child molestation case featured prominently in the news. "I'll tell you what needs to be done with a person like that," he roared as he paced back and forth on the stage. "If I had my way, he'd be lined up and they would empty a shotgun into his chest!" Suddenly the crowd exploded; people leaped to their feet with a thunderous applause and shouted, "Amen."

My wife groaned, "O God, help us!" I was stunned, frozen where I stood. The spiritual shock of the evangelist's comments went deep. Our hearts were still tender from the hours we had just spent in the presence of the God who is *love*. Now we watched as more than fifteen thousand Christians cheered for the shooting of another human being whom God created! *No matter how awful this man's sin might have been,* I thought, *this is not what Jesus is about.* I had attended all kinds of church services in my life, but I had never experienced anything like this. The thought of the pulpit and a congregation being perverted like this absolutely took my breath away. The anger, venom, and vengeance on the screen before us were worlds apart from the Spirit of Jesus who prayed for those who were crucifying him.

The next thing I remember, Carol began sobbing and saying, "Please, Jim, turn it off. I can't watch anymore." I did as she asked and felt my tears welling up. *Is this what viewers around*

America need to hear? I thought. *With all the problems around us, how can this be the good news Jesus told us to spread?*

"Someone has to talk to him, Jim, before it's too late," Carol blurted out as I began turning out the lights. "Something is really wrong in his spirit, and he will hurt the cause of the gospel before it's all over."

"I know," I said. I had the same ominous feeling as my wife, but it seemed there was little we could do.

"Can't you talk to your friend who knows him pretty well?" Carol asked. "Maybe he can counsel or warn him before it's too late."

I lay in bed that night praying that somehow God would stop this brother in Christ from pursuing what seemed to be a self-destructive course. Carol and I talked about the situation during the next week, but I didn't feel right about approaching my friend and asking him to intervene with someone of world renown whom I had never even met.

Eight days later, Carol and I again talked about the televangelist. Was there anything we could do for him—anything God wanted us to do?

Suddenly I felt a strong, distinct prompting to call my friend. He had a national ministry as well, and I knew he had spoken several times at the televangelist's school. I quickly picked up the phone and dialed his home. He answered, and after brief greetings I nervously got to the point of my call. "I really don't know how to say this, brother, and I sure don't want to put pressure on our friendship, but Carol and I are really troubled about something."

I quickly summarized our special Sunday night service and the spiritual pain we had felt upon hearing the televangelist's raw remarks. I told my friend how deeply this had affected us and that we just couldn't put it aside. But the phone seemed to go dead on the other end as I rambled on. "Are you still there, brother?" I asked.

After a brief pause, he slowly and emotionally replied, "Go on, Jim."

"Well, that's really it. We're aware that you know him pretty well, and maybe there's something God would have you do. Somebody has to do something, or we feel he's going to self-destruct. Do you know what I mean?"

Again, there was a strange silence. I was almost sure I could hear quiet sobbing on the other end of the line. "Hey, maybe I'm calling at a bad time," I added nervously. "Maybe I shouldn't even be bothering you with stuff like this."

"Jim, I'm glad you called," my friend said. "God meant for us to talk right now."

He then told me that just ten days earlier he and his wife had visited the televangelist's school. My friend had gone there to preach and was alarmed by what he had seen and discerned. The pace and pressure were so overwhelming, the financial crush so phenomenal, and the broadcasting and crusade schedule so demanding that the televangelist had no time for spiritual priorities. My friend saw him becoming spiritually shallow. Careful Bible study, time alone with the Lord, time alone with his wife—these essentials were being overrun by a monstrous empire that demanded all of his time and energy. My friend returned home with a broken heart and warning signals sounding inside him.

But that wasn't all. While in prayer a few nights before my call, my friend felt God's Spirit come upon him. The Lord seemed to give him a prophetic word of warning for the televangelist. With godly fear and trembling, he wrote it out in a letter. The main thrust of the letter was, "Shut it down. God wants you to shut it all down no matter what the cost may be. Get back to prayer, the Word, your family—get back to God. Don't worry about the supposed cost of shutting everything down, because the cost will be greater if you don't go back to your spiritual roots of communion with God."

My friend said he had prepared the letter for mailing but told his secretary not to send it until he gave the word. He wanted to be sure the Spirit of God was leading him because he knew that the letter could cost him his friendship with the televangelist. As my friend prayed that night in his study, he asked God to give him a sign— some confirmation that sending the letter of warning was of the Lord. That's when the phone rang. There I was on the other end, bringing up the very same subject!

The letter was sent the next day, but the response was not encouraging. My friend was told that his discernment and "word from the Lord" were way off base. The televangelist could never think of "shutting it all down" because too much was at stake—too many cities and countries to reach, too many television contracts signed, too many crusades planned, too much money coming in daily—to think that God could ever say something as radical as "shut it all down!"

The televangelist never listened to our mutual friend whom God used to warn him of the perils ahead. Soon the day came when he probably wished he had listened, wished he had shut it all down. But by then it was too late. By then his name and picture were known around the world as a symbol of scandal and shame. The spiritual cancer that had been growing for a long time had finally claimed its victim. All the tears and public apologies came too late to stop his life from careening out of control. In the end, it was *all* shut down—the empire, the international television ministry, the massive crusades. It became part of one of the saddest religious stories of the twentieth century.

I was much younger then as I watched the story unfold before me. I knew of at least one hidden episode of God's efforts to save the televangelist before his nasty fall. God *is* faithful, and God *is* love. The problem was, God was speaking but nobody was listening.

The problem was, God was speaking but nobody was listening.

From beginning to end, the Word of God greatly emphasizes the need to listen. We all make mistakes, fail to do God's will perfectly, and even rebel against his commands. But when we refuse to listen to his voice of correction and direction, things can quickly reach critical mass.

I remember how true this was on the playgrounds of Brooklyn where I played as a kid. Basketball was my thing; I devoted myself to the game. When I began playing on the varsity team at Erasmus Hall High School—a school with a great basketball tradition—I noticed something odd right away. The guys I knew from the park could play really well, but they never made the team, which meant that receiving a college athletic scholarship was out of the question. Many of these talented guys had one main problem: they wouldn't listen. No coach was going to change anything about their game. No, sir! No one could tell them how to defend better, shoot more accurately, or rebound better. They were uncoachable. They wouldn't listen. So all their God-given talent and ability counted for nothing.

Every instructor knows the dilemma of having a student who won't yield. Every parent knows the pain of having a prodigal who must have his or her way. Where we see failure, wasted opportunities, and heartache, this fatal flaw is invariably present.

THE KING WHO STARTED WELL

It's not always easy to listen. King Amaziah is one of God's poster people for this kind of problem. He is the man who wouldn't listen. The strange thing is that Amaziah *did* listen at first. He listened very closely and obediently to the Word of the Lord when he began his reign as king of Judah.

> Amaziah was twenty-five years old when he became king, and he reigned in Jerusalem twenty-nine years.... He did

what was right in the eyes of the LORD, but not wholeheartedly. After the kingdom was firmly in his control, he executed the officials who had murdered his father the king. Yet he did not put their sons to death, but acted in accordance with what is written in the Law, in the Book of Moses, where the LORD commanded: "Fathers shall not be put to death for their children, nor children put to death for their fathers; each is to die for his own sins" (2 Chronicles 25:1–4).

After he was established on the throne, Amaziah had to take care of some unfinished business. His father, the late King Joash, had been assassinated, and it was Amaziah's duty to punish the men responsible for this vicious crime. Although he now had absolute power, Amaziah did not give in to the desire for unbridled vengeance by executing the assassins and their families. (This was a common practice during those rough-and-tumble days when royal power wreaked havoc among the peoples of the world.) Rather, King Amaziah heeded the commandment of God found in Deuteronomy 24:16. This commandment limited punishment, no matter how grievous the crime, to only the guilty parties, not their innocent children. So Amaziah listened well to the Word of the Lord.

Another challenge also lay before the king. After organizing and enlarging his army for a major campaign against the Edomites, Amaziah "hired a hundred thousand fighting men from Israel" (2 Chronicles 25:6) at the cost of almost four tons of silver! He believed that the three hundred thousand troops from Judah could only be strengthened by adding one hundred thousand mercenaries from the northern kingdom of Israel. Everyone knows that in war, more is better, right? Well, Amaziah found out that God's math was different from his.

A man of God came to him and boldly declared, "These troops from Israel must not march with you, for the LORD is not with Israel" (v. 7). The northern ten tribes of Israel had given themselves over to gross idolatry, and the anger of Jehovah hung over them. Because of this, Amaziah was forbidden to deploy their forces. If he used them, he was told, "God will overthrow you before the enemy." As the prophet revealed, "God has the power to help or to overthrow" (v. 8). In other words, more is less if God doesn't bless!

Amaziah was still troubled, though, by the almost four tons of silver that would be wasted if he dismissed the Israelite troops. "But what about the hundred talents I paid for these Israelite troops?" he asked. The prophet replied, "The LORD can give you much more than that" (v. 9). So the king obediently dismissed the mercenaries. He then led his smaller army—one that had God's blessing—to the Valley of Salt and routed the Edomites.

What joy there was among the troops of Judah that night as they celebrated their impressive victory! What wonderful lessons Amaziah teaches us as we watch him obeying not only the express commands of the Law of God but also the prophetic voice of the Spirit of God. The king's obedience to God's leading in a specific situation, even at great monetary loss, is a powerful example for us to follow. As the king listened and obeyed, God was faithful to fulfill his promise of victory and blessing.

IT'S UNBELIEVABLE — OR IS IT?

But a very odd thing happened to King Amaziah as he concluded his campaign against the Edomites. His attention was drawn to the idols that his defeated foes worshiped. What he did seems too unbelievable to be true: "When Amaziah returned from slaughtering the Edomites, he brought back the gods of the people of Seir. He set them up as his own gods, bowed down to them and burned sacrifices to them. The anger of the LORD burned against Amaziah" (2 Chronicles 25:14–15).

How could this happen to a man who was so blessed by God? The Law of God clearly forbids bowing down to any heathen idol. The Lord had repeatedly commanded his people to have no other gods before him (Exodus 20:3; Deuteronomy 5:7). These were the ABCs of religious instruction among the Israelites! But somehow Amaziah's sick fascination with Edomite idols closed his ears to the Word of the Lord. Maybe it was his successful reign thus far. Maybe it was his great victory over the Edomites. We don't know why, but for some reason the king of Judah stopped measuring his actions against the precepts of God's Word.

Things went from bad to worse, which is what usually happens when people turn their backs on God.

Things went from bad to worse, which is what usually happens when men and women turn their backs on God. While Amaziah burned sacrifices to these abominable idols, God's anger burned against the king's audacious sin. A prophet of the Lord immediately confronted Amaziah with a logical question straight from the throne of God: "Why do you consult this people's gods, which could not save their own people from your hand?" (2 Chronicles 25:15). In other words, God said, "Wake up, Amaziah! These are not only dumb idols, they are the 'loser gods' that did nothing for the Edomites whom I helped you defeat so decisively!" It is incredible how sinful disobedience blinds us to truth, even when it is staring us right in the face.

Amaziah then escalated his stubbornness by rejecting a prophetic message that was sent to save him from his own devices. While the prophet was still speaking, the king said to him, "Have we appointed you an adviser to the king? Stop! Why be struck down?" (v. 16). The man who once listened, childlike, to God's voice now arrogantly cut off the prophet's message and threatened to kill him if he went any further. Before he left, the unnamed prophet said something that I pray the Holy Spirit will help us all to remember: "I know that God has determined to destroy you, because you have done this and *have not listened* to my counsel" (v. 16).

That was the solemn verdict. Once Amaziah closed his ears to the voice of God, nothing in heaven or on earth could help him. He was doomed because he wouldn't listen.

Amaziah soon unwisely attacked the northern kingdom of Israel. But God's blessing was no longer on him, so his army was routed. Amaziah's victorious enemies broke down about six hundred feet of Jerusalem's walls, seized the gold and silver and sacred articles in the temple, and raided the palace treasury. Hostages were taken from among the people. In the end, the nation of Judah was bankrupt, the temple had been violated, and countless families mourned the loss of husbands and fathers they would never see again. This was the sad legacy of the king who wouldn't listen.

A GREAT TRAGEDY

The truth is, no matter how deep our sin is, no matter how far we have fallen, there is still hope if we will just listen to what God is saying. It is when we get so full of ourselves and too busy to stop and listen that we cut ourselves off from the one true Friend who can help us. Our shallowness and self-centeredness make us deaf to words that would bring healing and spiritual life. Even when God sends family members and friends to warn or correct us, our pride often makes us incapable of receiving help. "I thought you were my friend—how could you say that?" is our immature reaction that shows we have completely missed what God was trying to do.

While I was preparing this message on King Amaziah for a Sunday sermon, I spent days meditating and praying about the best way to preach it. Among other things, I asked the Lord to give me a powerful illustration about the horrible sin of not listening to him. I can't say I was ready for or happy with the answer he provided.

Barbara was just a child when I first met her. She was the daughter of a precious couple God sent to our church during the early days of our ministry. Her father was a former alcoholic whom Christ powerfully transformed into a faithful, praying servant of God. Carol and I shared many meals at his home. While we enjoyed rice and beans and other Puerto Rican dishes, Barbara played in the next room with our daughter, Chrissy, who was about the same age.

Years went by, and Barbara's parents decided to move first to Pennsylvania and later retired to Puerto Rico. But problems with Barbara disturbed their otherwise tranquil life.

Barbara showed a nasty streak of rebellion as a teenager, and it got worse as time went on. She became so full of herself, her opinions, and the determination to do her own thing that she barely resembled the sweet girl we had watched grow up. She wouldn't listen to anyone who offered counsel or correction. She told off her family, her youth leaders, and anyone else who seemed to get in her way. I remember one brief encounter I had with her. I was shocked at the hardness of her heart. Barbara believed she had *all* the answers, that was for sure.

After her parents relocated to Puerto Rico, Barbara moved in with a guy and had a couple of kids by him. Their relationship ended, and Barbara moved to another borough of New York City. She was thirty-one and had dropped off the radar screen . . . until the week I was preparing my sermon on King Amaziah.

In the middle of that week, one of my associate pastors put on my desk two articles from the newspapers. One was from the *New York Post*, another from the *Daily News*. These were not two-line news items but full-blown articles about a horrible crime. And there was Barbara's picture in the middle of the whole mess. She had moved in with a nineteen-year-old guy who obviously had serious problems. The newspaper reported that her three-and-a-half-year-old daughter had been found murdered in the squalid apartment the couple shared. The young man was under arrest without bail, and Barbara was being held in Rikers Island, a very scary prison in which no one would ever want to spend even one night.

So while I was preaching the message "The Man Who Wouldn't Listen" on Sunday, a frightened, heartbroken woman was sobbing in a lonely cell in Rikers Island. But out of this horrible nightmare of sin and spiritual darkness there came a shaft of light. Barbara began to listen, to remember truths about Jesus that were taught to her years ago.

Barbara was released on bail after her arrest and quickly made her way to the Brooklyn Tabernacle. We had the entire congregation pray for her during a Tuesday night prayer meeting as she cried out to God for mercy and pardon. It was a very moving moment as we heard her pray, "Jesus, please forgive me. Help me! Give me another chance."

Barbara later told me that everything started turning sour in her life when she turned away from Jesus. That's when she shut her ears to the truths she had heard growing up and to the loving people who had pleaded with her to turn back to God. Not listening led Barbara into horrible situations she never dreamed of.

In the meantime, the charges against Barbara were bumped up to something far more serious, so she was sent back to prison to await trial. As I write this book, she sits once again in Rikers Island waiting for the outcome of her case. We have many people praying that God will grant mercy toward her, but this one thing we know: Barbara is not alone—and she knows it, too. Once again she is enjoying the peace that comes from listening to the Lord.

Thank God for his amazing loving-kindness.

THE UNEXPECTED LETTER

Barbara wrote to me from prison as I was still writing this chapter. After reading her letter, I knew it should be included here. She agreed to share it with you, believing that God will use it to wake up someone else to the importance of listening to God. She doesn't want anyone else to experience the heartache and pain she has felt and caused.

Dear Pastor Cymbala,

When you get this letter, I pray that it finds you and your family in good health.

I received the copy of *Fresh Power* that you sent me. I just finished it, and it truly blessed me. Funny, because a few days ago I was praying and asking God how I was supposed to go on without my daughter. But after I read the chapter about the couple in Africa, it was almost as if God was saying, "There's your answer." I doubt if I would be saved today, even though this tragedy was so terrible, without it.

When God took my daughter, he reminded me about how much I loved him at one time, how I trusted and believed in him. I had forgotten, Pastor, all about that. Although my heart hurts because I can't be with her, I know that through her death many people will come to know the Lord. It has already started. I started having Bible studies here in Rikers Island almost every night, and God has brought girls to me left and right.

God has a purpose for me behind these walls, and although I truly hate it here God has made the time go by "better." That's not to say that I don't have my days, because the Lord knows I do. But I know that when I cry out to him he's right there reminding me that he's just a cry away.

Our Bible study has grown. It started with just me and another girl, and now we have about five people coming every night and others who come in just for a little while. You see, I never really understood that verse that says, "You can't serve two masters." Now I do understand it. Before I left the church, I was trying to serve two masters, and I couldn't. The narrow road wasn't as pleasing as that wide one. God is so good, though, because he saved me.

I remember as a little girl I wanted to do nothing but sing, read, and praise him. As I reflect, sitting in my cell, I can see Jesus just sitting there and waiting and waiting and waiting through every heartbreak, through every bad time, while I was getting high to try to forget everything I was going through. He just sat there waiting, almost saying to me, "Call out to me, Barbara. I'll help you. Just call to me." But I didn't. I was too busy. . . .

I don't ever want to have anything to do with anything or anyone that doesn't have to do with God. I worshiped too many other gods, Pastor Cymbala, and they got me to this point.

Anyway, I'm going to stop writing now. I'll call or write later because my pencil is coming to the end of its point. I'll be sending girls from here, Pastor Cymbala, to your church, so please accept them and show them the same love that you have shown me. I tell the girls here that the only way they can change and not go back to their old ways is if they let God be first and trust him for everything. I have told many of them to go and see you guys, and that you all will help them. I hope that's okay. A lot of girls here want to change, but when they get out they go right back to their old lives and surroundings. They really can't change unless God helps them. I hope it's okay that I'm referring them all to you. Please let me know.

Anyway, keep me in your prayers. If it's all right, can you send me something more to read? I would rather read godly things now than the filthy books that they pass around inside the prison here.

I love you. May God bless and keep you.

Barbara.

CULTIVATE A LISTENING HEART

The divine message that Isaiah spoke thousands of years ago applies at all times to all people: "*Listen, listen* to me, and eat what is good, and your soul will delight in the richest of fare. *Give ear* and come to me; *hear me*, that your soul may live" (Isaiah 55:2–3). The key to a blessed life is to have a listening heart that longs to know what the Lord is saying.

Think for a moment about the lack of blessing and the increasing hardness of heart in the lives of so many Christians across the country. This emptiness comes primarily from not listening to God. Consider, too, the countless, discouraged pastors who are engrossed in every new fad and formula that comes from men but who spend little time waiting on God, waiting to hear the Holy Spirit's directives for their ministries. God is a speaking, communicating God, but someone has to be listening on the other end.

God is a speaking, communicating God, but someone has to be listening on the other end.

Jesus wrote letters to seven different churches in the book of Revelation. The spiritual condition of each assembly was different, and therefore Christ's words were never the same as he addressed their unique situations. But it is noteworthy that he used the *same* phrase to close *all* seven letters: "He who has an ear, let him *hear* what the Spirit says to the churches" (Revelation 2–3).

The Holy Spirit still speaks vital messages to God's people today, but we must have tender, attentive hearts to hear what he is saying.

When was the last time you and I could say that we *heard* from God? This is not some far-out, fanatical mysticism; it is a life-and-death issue that will affect our lives here on earth and determine our eternal destiny. God is still pleading in countless ways, "Hear me, that your soul may live" (Isaiah 55:3). Don't all of us need to slow down and get quiet before him? What benefit is there in anything else if we are not hearing what our Creator is saying to us?

God's eyes still roam over the earth looking for attentive, submissive hearts so he can show himself strong and mighty on our behalf. Let's ask God for the blessing of a childlike heart such as young Samuel had, so that when the Lord calls our name we, too, can answer, "Speak, for your servant is listening" (1 Samuel 3:10).

Lord, *help us to have a listening heart that is soft and teachable. Save us from being so filled with ourselves that we can't hear you. Give us the grace to both listen and obey when you speak to us. Amen.*

TWO

ƖMITATING GOD

We have all heard the phrase "Imitation is the highest form of flattery," but we may not realize just how great a role imitation plays in our lives. Whether or not we are conscious of doing it, we often incorporate things that impress us deeply into our own behavioral patterns. Not only do young children use imitation to help them learn, but we adults continue to mimic, in one way or another, throughout our lives. The entire advertising industry is largely built on the premise that people will imitate the lifestyles and choices of those they admire and esteem. When a few high-profile athletes started wearing their baseball caps backwards, it wasn't long before millions of kids and adults were doing the same thing.

GILLY, MY HERO

As a kid growing up in Brooklyn, I watched my sports heroes very carefully. I knew how they walked, how they swung a bat, and how they shot a basketball. I took it all in. What I saw—and imitated—influenced how I played. If I really idolized someone, I would go to extremes in order to mimic him, even copying his idiosyncrasies.

Gilly was one of those heroes. Three or four years older than me, he wasn't a Mickey Mantle, Willie Mays, or Duke Snider—the center fielders for the Yankees, Giants, and Dodgers who all played in New York City while I was in grade school. All the kids in my neighborhood argued constantly about which of these three superstars was the best. Gilly was no major-league superstar, but he was the best stickball player on Parkside Avenue. (Stickball is a street version of baseball, and back then it was the biggest sport on the block.) *Nobody* was better than Gilly.

A couple of times I was lucky enough to play on Gilly's team in a stickball game, but for the most part I was too young to play with his group. So I stood on the sidelines and, like a hawk, watched every move he made. He batted left and threw right, which I couldn't do, but everything else he did I emulated—how he threw, how he ran, even how he followed through after swinging the broom handle we used as a bat. But I didn't stop with that.

You see, Gilly wore an ID bracelet on his wrist. ID bracelets were hot items for teenagers back then. Every time he threw, or swung, or ran hard, his loose-fitting ID bracelet would slide up his arm a bit. He would then shake his hand and lower arm back and forth in order to get the bracelet to slide back to his wrist. It was just a little thing, but he did it all the time. Throw a few pitches or swing hard at a pitched ball, then shake that hand and arm back and forth. Run really hard with his arm churning, then shake that bracelet back into place.

I wasn't even conscious that my mimicking of Gilly went overboard, but my mother was. One day she couldn't take it any longer. "Why," she asked, "are you shaking your hand and arm back and forth every thirty seconds or so?" I was imitating the actions of one of my boyhood idols, but I had no ID bracelet on my wrist! I think my mother began to wonder if I needed psychological counseling.

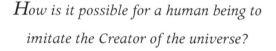

How is it possible for a human being to imitate the Creator of the universe?

For better or worse, we have all imitated other people. The apostle Paul recognized the power of imitation and used it in his teaching. In Ephesians 5:1 he commanded, "Be imitators of God, therefore, as dearly loved children." What exactly did he have in mind when he wrote that command? How is it possible for a human being to imitate the Creator of the universe who has all power, knows all things, and is present everywhere at the same time? It seems like much too tall an order for frail people like you and me who need God's help every moment of our lives. But the command still stands prominently in the Bible: "Be imitators of God!"

DAVID'S SPECIAL HEART

I believe imitating God, like listening to him, is another quality that aligns us with his purposes and makes room for even more of his blessings. Probably no one in the entire Old Testament illustrates this truth better than the king whom God called "a man after his own heart" (1 Samuel 13:14). David's imitation of God went to the very heart of the matter in more ways than one.

When David was young, his life was like a roller-coaster ride because of the opposition he faced. Although he slew Goliath, the Philistine giant, his fame among the Israelites made King Saul jealous rather than appreciative of him. Saul was consumed by his envy, and he ended up chasing David all over Israel in an attempt to kill him. Forced to live like a vagabond, David was separated from his wife, his parents, and his best friend. His life became a nightmare because of Saul's jealousy and vendetta against him. David wrote many of his psalms as he desperately tried to stay one step ahead of the bloodthirsty king and his formidable army.

But in the end, God's promise was fulfilled, and David sat on the throne of Israel (2 Samuel 5:3–4). He conquered Jerusalem and named it the City of David. Following that victory, he led successful campaigns against the Philistines, Moabites, and other enemies of Israel. David's fame spread everywhere, and his reign as king stands out as a glorious moment in Hebrew history.

At the very height of his power, David gives us a glimpse of his heart, that very special heart God treasured so dearly.

Summoning Ziba, a servant of the late King Saul, David asked, "Is there no one still left of the house of Saul to whom I can show God's kindness?" (2 Samuel 9:3). David's royal advisers and military leaders must have gasped when they heard the king's incredible question. *Kindness* and the name *Saul* did not belong in the same sentence! Saul, a madman, had fought against God's anointed for the throne. Saul had been full of evil. He broke promises. He was spiritually schizophrenic. He destroyed innocent people with no remorse. The only thing that Saul's family deserved was payback in full, right? How incredible it was for David, then, to search for ways in which to bless his archenemy's household and descendants!

Long before the new covenant was established, David experienced the new heart and new spirit God promised.

Clearly, the mercy and incredible favor God had shown to David remarkably affected the king's soul. Instead of spoiling for payback and harboring a spirit of vengeance, David's heart was filled with mercy and kindness, the very qualities God had demonstrated by promoting him so highly. David knew firsthand that Jehovah was the God of unmerited blessing and favor, so how could he not follow suit? Long before the new covenant was established, David experienced the new heart and new spirit God promised to give to true believers.

SERIOUS ISSUES

I wonder how many of us live stunted, narrow lives because we hold tightly to the record of wrongs committed against us? How much of our physical illness, chronic insomnia, or high anxiety is rooted in the memories of nasty rejections and painful hurts of years past? By not forgiving, by not letting these wrongs go, we aren't getting back at anyone. We are merely punishing ourselves by barricading our hearts, which are channels of God's grace. How can the Lord who delights in mercy (Psalm 25:6; Ephesians 2:4) walk with and abundantly bless a heart that is filled with resentment and unforgiveness? That is a spiritual impossibility because God cannot deny his nature. Is there a more solemn verse in the New Testament than Matthew 6:15: "But if you do not forgive men their sins, your Father will not forgive your sins"?

It is true that Saul's son, Jonathan, had been David's close friend. But that is not the primary motivation behind David's desire to show kindness. There is something far deeper at work here than granting a favor to a deceased friend. Note the question David asked: "Is there no one still left of the house of Saul to whom I can show

God's kindness?" It was God's kindness at work in David's heart that made him reach out to his enemies with mercy and blessing. He wouldn't give them what they "deserved" because God had not dealt with him in that manner.

The next time we are convinced of how right we are and how unjustly we have been treated, we would do well to remember this story. The next time we are certain that people *deserve* judgment and mustn't "get away" with the wrongs they have committed, let's each stop and think, *Is that how God has treated me?* If he reacted to our sins against him as we often react to the sins of those who offend us, where would we be today? The truth is, we have all been mercifully forgiven countless times in ways that no one but God knows. Yet how readily we react vehemently against those who have hurt us even once. We scream, "That was wrong!" and place the offender on the little "unforgiven" list we keep. How twisted is our sense of righteous indignation. That attitude is worlds apart from the cross of Christ, which is the source of our salvation.

Rather than remembering the wrongs committed against us, we would be far better off remembering this promise of Jesus: "Blessed are the merciful, for *they will be shown mercy*" (Matthew 5:7). Looking back over my life, all I can see is mercy and grace written in large letters everywhere. May God help me have the same kind of heart toward those who wound or offend me.

As it turns out, David's desire to be merciful was not for naught. There was one survivor from Saul's family to whom David could show kindness and mercy. Ziba informed the king that a son of Jonathan named Mephibosheth was living in Lo Debar. David quickly had him brought to Jerusalem.

SURPRISE!

Mephibosheth entered the king's palace trembling with fear. *What does King David want with me?* he no doubt wondered. *Theoretically, at least, I'm a threat to him. If public opinion shifts back in favor of the house of Saul, I would be the natural heir to the throne of Israel. Maybe David summoned me here because of my royal lineage. Maybe he wants to wipe out even the faintest threat to his throne.*

What a surprise Mephibosheth was in for. King David immediately calmed his fears: "'Don't be afraid,' David said to him, 'for I will surely show you kindness for the sake of your father Jonathan. I will restore to you all the land that belonged to your grandfather Saul, and you will always eat at my table'" (2 Samuel 9:7). Rather than choosing to destroy, David chose to bless. Instead of remembering Saul's evil deeds, King David mercifully restored to Saul's grandson all the land Saul had owned. David also commanded Ziba, as well as the servant's sons and servants, to farm the land for Mephibosheth. No wonder David was called a man after God's own heart! He delighted in mercy rather than judgment.

We also read that "Mephibosheth lived in Jerusalem, because he always ate at the king's table, and he was crippled in both feet" (v. 13). What a beautiful picture of the way God deals with everyone who trusts in his Son, Jesus Christ. We not only receive mercy and pardon, but we are called into fellowship by the very One we have sinned against! From that day forward, Mephibosheth always ate at the king's table so that David could provide for him daily and so that he could enjoy the king's presence. How incredible is the kindness of the Lord, and how blessed David was for imitating so well the heart of God!

BECOMING WHOLE

It is interesting to discover how poor Mephibosheth became crippled. He was only five years old when the news came from Jezreel that the Philistines had routed Israel and that both Saul and Jonathan had been killed. During the panic of the moment, "his nurse picked him up and fled, but as she hurried to leave, he fell and became crippled" (2 Samuel 4:4). Mephibosheth was damaged for life because someone accidentally dropped him. For the rest of his life, he could not work. He could not hike in the countryside, train for battle, or hold his own in a crowd. He had to rely on the compassion or pity of others just to survive. Yet, years later he was given a position of honor—all because God's kindness and mercy flowed from the heart of David.

These details about Mephibosheth give us another valuable point to consider. Many people act the way they do because at some time someone "dropped" them accidentally or purposely. I don't write this to rationalize their behavior or excuse their sins, but it is a fact we must keep in mind because it impacts their spiritual life. Not everyone has had the family support and other advantages with which some of us have been blessed. I counsel many people whose lives read like some kind of horror story. They have been damaged, yet God extends his kindness and mercy to them despite their crippled conditions. In fact, God is drawn to people who have deep needs. He desires to make them whole and to wash away every stain of their sin (Psalm 51:7; Isaiah 1:18). God invites them to sit at his table even though they still exhibit a "spiritual limp" that has not yet healed. He is always ready to meet people wherever they are, no matter how dreadful their sins may seem. Steven Langella knows this truth well.

God is always ready to meet people wherever they are, no matter how dreadful their sins may seem.

SEEKING AN ESCAPE

Steven was born in New York City into a typical, middle-class home. His dad was a longshoreman, and his mom stayed at home to raise the children. It was a traditional Catholic home, and he attended parochial rather than public schools. While Steven was still a boy, his parents started having marital problems. At that time his mother began an affair with a former New York City cop and Marine who stood 6-foot-3 and weighed about 220 pounds. Eventually his parents divorced, ending the relatively normal and happy life Steven had enjoyed.

The following year, Steven's mother picked up the family and moved to Florida with her boyfriend. Steven's father wasn't even aware his children were gone. This brought chaos and deep emotional pain to all the kids. The new "family" settled into a shabby little house that was very different from their former home on Staten Island. This was but one of many changes Steven faced.

Steven's stepfather was a hard man who seemed to have little patience with him. For years he routinely beat the boy, called him names, and threatened to send him away from his mother. When he was eleven, Steven had his first encounter with pornography when his brother showed him a *Playboy* magazine. This planted a deadly seed that would yield much horrible fruit during the years to come. Steven recounts what happened later:

"At the age of seventeen, I decided to join the army. Soon I was doing my basic training at Fort Gordon in Georgia. I found out quickly that the army presented some real problems for me. All those officers talking down to me reminded me of my stepfather. It seemed like I was always getting into trouble, and I barely made it through basic training. In the army I was exposed to more pornography and started going to strip clubs. Then I had my first sexual encounter with a prostitute. I had always been shy with girls, but now pornography, prostitutes, and strip clubs became an escape for me. I found acceptance there, and it seemed like someone actually showed affection to me."

At eighteen, Steven was kicked out of the army. For the next six years he moved about, living in several states while working as a bartender. He stayed only a few months in any one place. During that time he had a few girlfriends but no meaningful relationships—and he became more engrossed in pornography and sexual promiscuity. Eventually he took a job as a merchant seaman and traveled all over the world. This lifestyle aggravated his problems, and he wasted all of his money on partying and prostitutes.

Eventually Steven ended up back in Brooklyn, where he again worked as a bartender. There he couldn't help but notice a change in the life of one of his friends.

"Paul had been the biggest drunk in the neighborhood," Steven recalls. "He would start fights all the time, and if things went bad he sometimes would return with a shotgun. But now he was totally different. Paul shared with me about the love of Jesus. The change in him was so radical and obvious that, simply out of curiosity, I finally agreed to go to church with him one Sunday. During the service, a simple gospel message was preached. The speaker said that God has a plan for every person and that to reject Jesus Christ was to choose hell over heaven and death over life. I knew my life was twisted and wrong, so on that Sunday morning I put my faith in Jesus Christ as Savior."

TEMPTATION

Steven soon began attending the Brooklyn Tabernacle, where he served as an usher and in other ministries. God had changed his life, and through Steven's influence all three of his sisters received Christ within the next few years. But the battle for his soul was far from over. He began to struggle once again with lustful passions.

"One night in 1989 as I was watching television," he told me, "a commercial came on with a very sexy woman dressed in lingerie lying on a sofa. 'Hi, my name is Amber,' she said. 'Call me right now and meet some of my beautiful friends.' This was her come-on, and I immediately began to struggle with this new temptation. I finally gave in and called the 900 number and learned that I could meet women in the New York City area. I ended up speaking with someone whom I later met. We got involved sexually, and afterward I felt so convicted and miserable. Upon returning home that night, I fell on my face and sobbed uncontrollably. The next Sunday I asked God for his forgiveness and promised not to do that again. But the 900-number seduction was very powerful. An enormous battle began raging within me, and soon I was back on the phone again. No matter how many promises I made to God, no matter how many tears I cried, I could not seem to get victory over this area of temptation."

During the next few years, Steven's spiritual life went up and down like a yo-yo. Victory lasted for a few weeks or months, followed by a fall back into the pit. Discouragement and fatigue set in, so Steven tried to run away. He took a job as a merchant seaman again and ended up on a cargo ship seven thousand miles away in the Persian Gulf.

By this time the spiritual battle he faced seemed hopeless. Feeling as if he had crossed a line with God, Steven became convinced that the Lord was through with him and was no longer concerned about his polluted life. But soon Steven would find himself echoing these words of David, who also experienced moral failure:

Where can I go from your Spirit?
Where can I flee from your presence?
If I go up to the heavens, you are there;
if I make my bed in the depths, you
are there.
If I rise on the wings of the dawn,

> if I settle on the far side of the sea,
> even there your hand will guide me,
>> your right hand will hold me fast
> (Psalm 139:7–10).

Steven Langella may have given up on himself, but God had not given up on Steven Langella.

Steven Langella may have given up on himself, but God had not given up on Steven Langella.

"One day, as I walked out onto the deck of the ship to watch the sunset, a deckhand was sitting nearby smoking a cigarette. I remarked casually that the sunset was especially beautiful, but was stunned by his reply. 'Yes, it is, but I still don't like the fact that the people around here don't believe in Jesus. I know I'm not living right, but I believe that Jesus Christ is the only way. One day I'm going to give my life to him.'

"Here was a foulmouthed merchant seaman on a ship in the Persian Gulf telling me about Jesus! Immediately a deep conviction settled over my heart. I couldn't shake it off. At two o'clock the next morning, I awoke from a deep sleep in total darkness. I was disoriented and had no idea where I was. Suddenly the thought of spending eternity in the darkness of hell overwhelmed me. I began screaming and crawling on the floor. Then I banged my head against a bulkhead. In my agony I began crying and begging God to leave me alone. But the Lord did not abandon me. Instead, he reminded me of his love and mercy. He could have blasted me off the planet, but he kept reaching out in tenderness and compassion."

Steven returned to Brooklyn and began to learn how to live in victory. Instead of depending on his strength or personal resolve, he yielded his problems and his life wholly to the Lord. He discovered that God is the only One who can heal the crippled areas of a person's life. Faith in Christ is the victory that overcomes not only the world but every engrained sin of the flesh. It doesn't matter how far we have gone, or how deeply the stains of sin have penetrated—

the mercy of God is unlimited in its power and scope.

Today when Steven shares his testimony of deliverance, he focuses on God's relentless love and mercy. One of the most spiritually minded men in our church, he is no longer addicted to pornography, and God's hand is upon him. We are excited to see what his future in Christ holds.

THE ONLY CURE

Although our life stories are different, don't we all come from the same pit of sin from which Steven was rescued? Is there one of us today who cannot identify with these words from the apostle Paul? "At one time *we too* were foolish, disobedient, deceived and enslaved by all kinds of passions and pleasures. We lived in malice and envy, being hated and hating one another. But when the kindness and love of God our Savior appeared, he saved us, not because of righteous things we had done, but because of his mercy" (Titus 3:3–5). No matter what our individual stories may be, we can all recite one Scripture passage in unison as our collective testimony: "Because of the LORD's great love we are not consumed, for his compassions never fail. They are new every morning; great is your faithfulness" (Lamentations 3:22–23).

Understanding God's heart of love and compassion is crucial for the believer because it is the very foundation of our salvation through Jesus Christ. But there is more: God's compassions are "new every morning." We must appropriate the tender mercy of God every day *after* conversion or problems will quickly develop. We need his grace daily in order to live a righteous life.

We must appropriate the tender mercy of God every day after conversion or problems will quickly develop.

Consider, for a moment, the massive invasion of pornography into the Christian church, especially the inroads being made into the ministry. The battles that Steven Langella fought are being duplicated in many lives. Attempting to fight this sin, some preachers emotionally stir up and motivate people to make new, more earnest vows and promises to change their sinful ways. But like Steven, who tried so hard to change his ways through his own strength and still ended up spiritually beaten and discouraged, many Christians across the land are losing the battle and living with secret shame and hopeless despair.

We must recognize that when we face deeply rooted habits of sin in daily spiritual warfare, self-help is no help at all. There is only one cure, and it comes from God.

God has promised not to leave us alone in our confusion and weakness. He offers an answer, his *only* answer: "For the grace of God that brings salvation has appeared to all men. It teaches us to say 'No' to ungodliness and worldly passions, and to live self-controlled, upright and godly lives in this present age" (Titus 2:11–12).

Notice that *only* the grace of God can teach us to say, "No!" properly and effectively. All the human resolve we can muster and all the well-intentioned promises we can make are utterly powerless against the strength of fleshly desires. It is only as God's Spirit works within us "to will and to act accordingly to his good purpose" (Philippians 2:13) that we can experience daily victory over every besetting sin.

So God's heart of mercy provides for us not only pardon from sin but a daily provision of spiritual food to strengthen us. Even as crippled Mephibosheth sat daily at King David's table, let us take our seats and avail ourselves of every mercy and blessing God sets before us. There, in the presence of the eternal and sovereign King, we can "receive mercy and find grace to help us in our time of need" (Hebrews 4:16).

Father, we bring all our failures to you in Jesus' name. We have tried so hard and so often to change. But our problems are too big for us to handle. Today, we give up and throw ourselves totally on your love and mercy. Cleanse us and change us from the inside out. Teach us how to imitate you—to have your heart of kindness and mercy. Teach us to walk in the Spirit every day so we can know your power and victory. We rest in your mercy and faithfulness. Amen.

THREE

WHEN BLESSING BECOMES A CURSE

Years ago when I was a boy, there was a popular television show called *The Millionaire*. Every week a new episode featured a fictitious plot in which the same anonymous donor picked someone at random to receive one million dollars each. The stories then revealed the incredible changes that the unexpected, enormous gift created in the life of the recipient and other people around him or her.

You would think that everything turned out great for the person who received this money, but that wasn't always the case. Often the gift transformed the recipient into someone who was very ugly, which made for a fascinating story line but a sad reality.

We can see numerous examples from real life that reveal this same chain of events. A person wins the lottery and suddenly has millions of dollars at his or her disposal. An athlete works hard and emerges as a superstar; money, fame, and media exposure almost make him a one-man industry. In both cases, the story does not always have a beautiful ending. We often learn that what seems to be colossal good fortune can turn strangely and quickly into a story of human tragedy.

PROMISING BEGINNINGS

The Word of God is filled with stranger story lines than any we see on television or read about in the newspapers. It reveals that sometimes even God's choicest blessings upon his people can produce unexpected and tragic results.

In chapter 1 we learned about Amaziah, the man who wouldn't listen. After Amaziah was assassinated, his sixteen-year-old son, Uzziah, ascended the throne. Many commentators believe Uzziah actually became king while his idol-worshiping father was living out the last years of his tragic life.

In the same way that people who strike it rich or achieve stardom appear to have a bright future, Uzziah's reign began with great success and promise. A long, uninterrupted series of victories and national improvements spread his fame all the way to Egypt. He began by wisely recapturing and rebuilding the important city of Elath in southern Judah, which greatly enhanced the nation's opportunity for trade and commerce. Uzziah then orchestrated successful military ventures against the Philistines, Arabians, and Meunites. Even the powerful Ammonites were forced to pay tribute to Uzziah.

Not content with these victories, the king expanded and reorganized his army in order to achieve greater efficiency. With the help of resourceful men, he invented new war machines (probably along the line of catapults) that could hurl arrows and large rocks at opposing armies with greater force and accuracy. He also fortified strategic cities, making Judah almost impregnable.

But Uzziah was more than just a military leader. He oversaw the vast enterprises of livestock and farming that prospered during his reign. He "dug many cisterns, because he had much live-stock in the foothills and in the plain. He had people working his fields and vineyards in the hills and in the fertile lands, for he loved the soil" (2 Chronicles 26:10). Fields and vineyards, hills and fertile lands were all affected by his progressive programs and love for the land. Uzziah was no narrow-minded man; he was a king noted for his diverse interests and unusual intelligence.

WHAT'S THE SECRET?

Do you know the secret behind Uzziah's ability to succeed in everything he endeavored to do? The Bible gives the exact, very simple reason for Uzziah's success: "God helped him" (2 Chronicles 26:7). A few verses later, to be more emphatic, the Word of God declares that "he was greatly helped" (v. 15). Some translations render this phrase "marvelously helped."

The word translated "help" in both these verses comes from a Hebrew root that means "surrounded." Whatever challenges or battles King Uzziah faced, God surrounded him with a wall of blessing. No matter which angle anyone took to attack Judah, or which difficulties arose, the Lord was there to help this extraordinary king. To attack Uzziah meant you had to take on God first!

God's blessing was the secret behind all of Uzziah's success. But was there a reason why God showed him such unusual favor? The Bible clearly affirms that the events leading to Uzziah's success were not accidents of providence—such things do not exist in the spiritual realm. Rather, they were the result of something Uzziah was habitually doing. Scripture reveals that "he [Uzziah] continued to seek God in the days of Zechariah, who had understanding through the vision of God; and *as long as he* [Uzziah] *sought the Lord*, God prospered him" (2 Chronicles 26:5 NASB).

As long as the heart of Uzziah humbly sought the Lord, God prospered him.

The Hebrew word translated "prospered" actually means "to push ahead." As long as the king humbly looked to God for guidance and protection, he was pushed forward, surrounded, helped, and blessed by the Almighty. Who would not want to live as the object of that kind of a smile from heaven?

Note also the time period during which Uzziah was seeking God and enjoying such divine favor. It was "in the days of Zechariah, who had understanding through the vision of God." This Zechariah was not the prophet whose book is included among the books of the Minor Prophets in our Bible. This Zechariah was another servant of the Lord who was also in touch with heaven and the invisible things of the Spirit. Zechariah's friendship and influence were important to Uzziah because it was the prophet who kept stirring Uzziah to seek the Lord, which in turn brought the king success in everything he did.

OUR NEED FOR "ZECHARIAHS"

What a blessing it is to have a Zechariah in your life! Do you have a spiritually minded friend who reminds you of the greatness of God and his promises? Do you have someone who stirs within you a spiritual hunger for more of God? We all need more than polite acquaintances or friends who share similar interests. In the day in which we live, we urgently need Zechariahs—people who encourage and inspire us to move toward God and away from the world's enticing pleasures.

We urgently need Zechariahs—
people who encourage and inspire us
to move toward God.

I am thankful that I am blessed with Zechariahs in my life. One of my ministerial friends from another part of the country speaks with me by telephone about once a week. Our family picture sits on his desk, and he prays for us daily. Every time I hang up the phone after talking with him, I want to know my Bible better, get closer to God, and preach more effectively for Christ.

Often God uses man's words to bless me and even to provide answers to situations I am facing.

HIDE-AND-SEEK?

As we consider the importance of Uzziah's "seeking the Lord" and how it led to God's blessing, perhaps we should take a closer look at what this familiar phrase really means. Was the Lord playing hide-and-seek with Uzziah? Is that why Uzziah had to *seek* him? Was God trying to be elusive? What did the Lord mean when he spoke these words through the prophet Jeremiah: "You will seek me and find me when you seek me with all your heart" (Jeremiah 29:13)?

Seeking God is not merely an Old Testament concept; it is at the heart of every real relationship with the Almighty "because anyone who comes to him [God] must believe that he exists and that *he rewards those who earnestly seek him*" (Hebrews 11:6).

The question is not whether you attend church or how many Bible verses you know. Those things, although important, do not necessarily make us seekers after God. Neither does calling ourselves Baptists, Presbyterians, fundamentalists, evangelicals, or charismatics. God is not interested in how many *seeker-sensitive* churches there are but in how many *seeking* churches there are and how many people have *seeking* hearts like that of young King Uzziah.

Under Zechariah's godly influence, Uzziah was doing two essential things. First, he was *seeking help from Almighty God*. The king was conscious of his weakness and his inability to rule Judah rightly in his own strength. He knew that he needed God's direct assistance. This humble recognition of need is at the heart of all real prayer and provides the motivation for spending time in God's presence. The word translated "sought" in 2 Chronicles 26:5 actually means "to tread or frequent" a certain place. It is sometimes translated in the King James Version as "to question" or "to require." Uzziah must have spent much time with the Lord because his tender heart knew no other source of help. How much we need to follow his example by praying every day, "Oh, Lord, I need your help. I can't make it without you."

As he sought God, Uzziah was seeking not only the Lord's help but also his approval. Desiring God's approval is the other half of the seeking that brought Uzziah such blessing during the days of Zechariah. Although many people run to church or say prayers when they are in trouble, they may give little thought to having a life that is pleasing to the Lord—to find out what delights *him!* They may think of God as "an ever-present help in trouble" (Psalm 46:1), but all too often they put him out of their minds as soon as the crisis is over. Real seeking of God involves searching God's Word to learn the things that bring him joy. Uzziah was not too concerned about what made other people happy. Like David, he was far more concerned that the words of his mouth and the meditations of his heart would be acceptable to God (Psalm 19:14). "He did what was right in the eyes of the LORD" (2 Chronicles 26:4). Uzziah's humble heart was not bent on sinful self-seeking but rather on pleasing God, and this is what brought heaven's favor upon him.

UNEXPECTED RESULTS

At the end of our lives, what will it matter how popular or well liked we were? We will all stand before the Lord, and it will be his judgment alone that will matter. That is why we repeatedly read in the books of Kings and Chronicles that the kings did right or evil "in the eyes of the Lord." What the people felt or how other nations viewed them was insignificant. It was Almighty God's verdict that determined the course of their history.

Seeking after God is a two-pronged endeavor. It requires not only the humility to say, "God, I need you," but also a heart that desires a pure life that is pleasing to the Lord. As long as King Uzziah sought God in both these ways, it was impossible for anyone or anything to bring him down.

It would be nice if the story of Uzziah ended here, but the Bible is an honest book. Uzziah's life took a sudden dive, and the cause of his downfall is amazing:

> His fame spread far and wide, for he was greatly helped *until* he became powerful. But after Uzziah became powerful, *his pride* led to his downfall. He was unfaithful to the LORD his God and entered the temple of the LORD to burn incense on the altar of incense (2 Chronicles 26:15–16).

Uzziah's heart became proud, so he lost the favor of God. His arrogance caused him to think he could do anything he wanted—even usurp the role of the priests, the only ones whom God authorized to enter the Holy Place to burn incense on the golden altar.

It is ironic that what led to his heart being lifted up with pride was the blessing of God! Uzziah was helped by the Lord so much that he became extremely powerful. He commanded a huge army. He had vast vineyards and farmlands, countless sheep and cattle, and smart men helping him; his fame had spread everywhere. But instead of being humbled by all those blessings and thanking God for them, Uzziah began to think that *he* had had something to do with getting them. The king of Judah lost sight of what had made him strong in the first place. It all went to his head. He began to believe that it was *his* talent and *his* leadership that had accomplished so much.

As always, pride came before a terrible fall.

A STRONG WARNING

Uzziah's story sends a warning to us all. Many times I have seen a similar progression played out before me. A young couple walk humbly before the Lord and seek God with all their heart. They can't afford a decent reception on their wedding day, but they do have peace and joy in Jesus. They pray about everything: "Oh, God, we need you. We want your will done in our lives. Please help us. We know that every good thing comes from you."

As time goes by, God's favor fills their lives with many good things. But they allow the blessings of God to turn their eyes away from the Giver; they become preoccupied with the gifts. Soon their tenderness of heart vanishes. They don't have time for God. They become filled with themselves and lose that special touch of God on their life together.

Blessings can either humble us and draw us closer to God, or allow us to become full of pride and self-sufficiency.

How we respond to the Lord's blessings makes all the difference. The blessings can either humble us and draw us closer to God, or they can lift us up and allow our hearts to become full of pride and self-sufficiency.

Look back over church history, and you will see the cycle of humility . . . prayer . . . blessing . . . pride . . . downfall . . . repeated over and over again. Pastors, churches, and denominations begin in lowliness and fervent seeking of God and his blessings. But years later, the very successes God has granted have become stumbling blocks, causing them to drift away from the godly, Holy Spirit-directed road on which they began.

God knew from the beginning how blessings could become a curse, so he had Moses warn the Israelites before they entered the land of Canaan:

> Be careful that you do not forget the LORD your God, failing to observe his commands, his laws and his decrees that I am giving you this day. Otherwise, when you eat and are satisfied, when you build fine houses and settle down, and when your herds and flocks grow large and your silver and gold increase

and all you have is multiplied, then your heart will become proud and you will forget the LORD your God, who brought you out of Egypt, out of the land of slavery. . . . *You may say to yourself, "My power and the strength of my hands have produced this wealth for me."* But remember the LORD your God, for it is he who gives you the ability to produce wealth, and so confirms his covenant, which he swore to your forefathers, as it is today (Deuteronomy 8:11–14, 17–18).

Imagine the danger of it! The answers to our prayers can cause our hearts to become proud and stop humbly seeking the Lord.

This tendency to become proud after receiving the blessings of God predates Moses' warning to the Israelites. It had its beginning before the earth itself was created. Lucifer was the most beautiful of all the created angelic beings (Ezekiel 28), but it was that beauty —a special gift from God—that lifted his heart against the Lord. There was no devil to tempt him. It was his rebellion against God that caused him to be cast out of heaven, and it was then that he became Satan, our adversary.

No wonder "God opposes the proud but gives grace to the humble" (James 4:6). The stench of pride in God's nostrils reminds him of the sin that rocked heaven itself and caused a rebellion among his angelic host. The Bible never says that God *resists* a drunkard, a thief, or even a murderer, but he *does resist* the proud. Every kind of sin can be cleansed and forgiven if we humble ourselves and confess it to the Lord. But pride has a devilish quality that keeps us from sensing our need for God's grace.

Pride has a devilish quality that keeps us from sensing our need for God's grace.

This awful sin of arrogant independence had infected the heart of King Uzziah. But he was about to learn another truth of Scripture: "Those who walk in pride he [God] is able to humble" (Daniel 4:37).

CONSEQUENCES

As he foolishly entered the temple to offer incense to God—something God had forbidden him to do—Uzziah was confronted by very brave priests. They told him, "Leave the sanctuary, for you have been unfaithful; and you will not be honored by the LORD God" (2 Chronicles 26:18). But it is very rare for a proud heart to heed correction. After all, he was King Uzziah—master builder, trader, organizer, and conqueror, famous throughout the world. Nobody was going to tell *him* what to do!

King Uzziah did not have the last word, though. The Scripture says that "while he was raging at the priests . . . in the LORD's temple, leprosy broke out on his forehead" (v. 19). The priests hustled him out of the Holy Place, but it was too late. Uzziah had leprosy until the day he died. For many years he was forced to live apart from society, temple worship, and his family. Even his death was pitiful. Despite all that he had accomplished, he couldn't be buried with the other kings in the royal cemetery. In fact, the last words spoken about him in the narrative are "he had leprosy" (v. 23). The king whose spiritual life began so beautifully ended up losing God's favor, and his fall served as a warning to the entire nation of Judah. As King David had written hundreds of years earlier, "Though the LORD is on high, he looks upon the lowly, but the proud he knows from afar" (Psalm 138:6). Jehovah is able to discern very clearly between a proud spirit and a humble heart.

A HUGE IMPRESSION

I was about seven years old when an unusual man of God spoke at the midweek service of the small church my parents were attending. His name was Howard Goss, and I will never forget the impression he left on my young heart. He was a huge man with a bald head and hands the size of baseball gloves. I never paid much attention to Bible preachers back then, but this man captured my interest. This large, gentle minister radiated something I had never felt before.

Howard Goss didn't rant and rave to make his point. Nor did he use any emotional gimmicks as he delivered the Word of God. He simply explained the truths of Scripture in an easy, conversational tone. But he also conveyed an unusual sense of the blessing of God, a fact I grew to appreciate much later in life.

I had been in the ministry for about six years when I visited the city of Manila in the Philippines to speak at a large church celebrating its anniversary. As I browsed in the pastor's study before the service, I noticed a book written by Howard Goss many years earlier. He had died since I had last seen him, but I still vividly remembered the impression he made on me.

The pastor noticed the book I was leafing through and abruptly exclaimed, "You know, his son goes to church here."

"What, here in Manila?" I asked.

"Yeah, he lived away from God for many years, went through a divorce, and ended up in the Philippines. He's married to a Filipino woman, and their two boys go to church with him all the time."

There was plenty of time before the service began, so I asked if I could meet him. Within minutes a tall, hulking, middle-aged man walked in—the exact double of his late father, complete with the large, balding head and huge hands. I was stunned by the uncanny resemblance. As we sat and talked, I explained my interest in knowing more about his dad. He told me about his father's conversion, long years of preaching ministry, and beautiful marriage. Then he opened up to me even more:

"Even though I drifted away from God, I never could get away from my parents' prayers," he told me. "The farther I strayed, the more they interceded for me. Dad was always seeking God. I would so often see him on his knees in his study. His heart was so sincere before the Lord that I couldn't take being around him when I was living so terribly. One night he and Mom prayed a long time for me and waited up until I got home from my carousing.

"'Son, you're coming back to the Lord!' they said. 'God assured us in prayer tonight that it's just a matter of time. Hallelujah!' And they were right, as usual. I ran for a long time, but the Lord just got me into a corner and that was it. I surrendered my life back to him years ago, and my two boys are now fine young men of God. I just wish my dad had seen with his own eyes the answer to his prayers.

"You know, Pastor, my dad really walked with God. He was so unusual compared to most of the ministers I saw while growing up. He was quite famous in his circle of churches, and everybody wanted him to speak, especially at those huge summer-camp meetings. He was a good writer and became an elder statesman to a multitude of younger preachers and congregations. But all the acclaim and popularity, all the invitations and compliments, never affected him except to make him more humble before God.

"I'll never forget one big camp meeting up in Canada when I was a kid. Every famous preacher was invited, and the crowds were tremendous. Our family arrived a day early, and the leaders were making out the schedule for the speakers. Meetings were held all day long—morning, afternoon, and night—and the visiting preachers all wanted to speak during the night rallies when the crowds were largest. The preachers actually jockeyed around, hoping to get the biggest meetings for their preaching assignments.

"Suddenly one of the leaders asked where my father was. He was in the prime of his ministry and was highly respected by everyone.

They wanted to consult with him, but no one seemed to know where he was. They finally heard that he was last seen in the kitchen and dining hall area, so I went with them to find him.

"They could scarcely believe their eyes when they got to the kitchen. There was my dad on his hands and knees scrubbing the floor with some of the other workers!

"'Brother Goss,' they said, 'what are you doing here? We're making out the preaching schedule and wanted to know your preference.'

"'Oh, brothers,' my dad replied, 'you've got so many good preachers here that you don't need to worry about me. But I found out that they're short of help here in the kitchen so I thought I'd lend a hand.'"

Tears welled up in our eyes as the son reminisced about his father, whose godly heart had left such a deep impression on so many.

"My dad was sure different, Pastor," he said. "He was the real thing. His heart was so humble before the Lord that he had a special power in prayer and in preaching. The Lord was really with my dad."

A humble heart is like a magnet that draws the favor of God toward us.

God can be with you and me in the same way as we walk with humble hearts before him. Just as pride drives away the blessings of heaven and precedes certain failure, a humble heart is like a magnet that draws the favor of God toward us. The Lord really does dwell with certain people in a special way. He is there because of the resting place provided for him by their humble hearts. It is a kind of divine favoritism verified by the Word of God. "This is what the LORD says: 'Heaven is my throne, and the earth is my footstool. Where is the house you will build for me? *Where will my resting place be?* . . . This is the one I esteem: *he who is humble* and contrite in spirit, and trembles at my word'" (Isaiah 66:1–2).

Let us humble our hearts before the Lord and seek his help and approval above all other things. Then by his grace we will personally experience the awesome power of his might as he surrounds us with blessings and favor. God will act in keeping with his promise: "Humble yourselves, therefore, under God's mighty hand, that *he may lift you up* in due time" (1 Peter 5:6).

Father, help us to humble ourselves before you. Save us from the pride and arrogance that cuts us off from your hand of blessing. Teach us to walk softly each day before you and to never lose sight of your greatness and our need. Amen.

FOUR

LOOKING UP

Every Tuesday night at the Brooklyn Taberna-cle, we conduct the most important service of the entire week—our prayer meeting. We pastors look forward to it more than anything else on the church calendar. The building is so jam-packed with people that we have to use the platform, choir risers, lobby area, and an overflow room to fit everyone in. Often people can't find a seat any-where, so they stand during the entire meeting, which is filled with worship, prayer, petition, and intercession. When you think about it, there is a lot to pray for, and there is a God in heaven whose ear is always open to the cries of his people.

Helping us each Tuesday night is the Brooklyn Tabernacle Prayer Band. Founded by Pastor Kenneth Ware, one of my associates, the Prayer Band devotes itself to bringing prayer requests from all over the city, country, and world to the throne of grace. Pastor Ware has been greatly used by God to inspire members of our congregation to give themselves to this vital ministry. Every hour of every day of the year, Prayer Band members are interceding in our prayer room. They volunteer on a scheduled rotation so that every emergency request can be responded to immediately—day or night.

During the Tuesday night service, Prayer Band members sit together like a small army on the choir risers behind me, ready to serve the pastors and congregation. The service ends informally because we encourage people to linger as long as they want to and keep praying. The people who have to leave do so, but everyone knows the building will stay open as long as necessary, even if a person wants to join the Prayer Band members during their overnight shifts.

During these "after-service" times, I regularly sit with the Prayer Band and wait before the Lord with them. Each week brings new challenges, so I need to talk to God about many things. During much of the prayer service, I lead the congregation in prayer for others. Afterwards, I try to focus on my own needs.

About two years ago, I took my seat among the Prayer Band members and asked five or six of them to pray for me. I opened my heart to the Lord as they gently laid hands on my shoulders.

After a while, I heard a female voice among them intercede for me. As the woman led out in prayer, I discerned that her whole heart was in it and that the Holy Spirit was helping her. Her prayer was fervent, bold, and scriptural. She quoted promise after promise from God's Word. As she continued in prayer, she began asking the Lord to help and strengthen me in areas that no one could know about but God and me. She seemed to read right into my heart and life as she pleaded, asking God to help this frail man who was her pastor. I wept openly as she led us to the throne of heaven, where God so readily provides his mercy and grace.

Who is this woman who prays with such spiritual insight and faith? I wondered. I didn't recognize her voice, and I never looked around to see who she was. During subsequent weeks, however, the same thing happened two more times. A group around me was praying when suddenly that same voice interceded. It was as if she could not be denied. I don't know all the members of the Prayer Band personally, but I finally discovered who God was using to bless me—a tall, slender, African-American woman in her mid-thirties. Her name is Silvia Glover.

If your back were against the wall, you would want Silvia Glover in your corner calling out to heaven.

You might be wondering what kind of spiritual roots a prayer warrior like Silvia must have. Which Bible seminary did she attend? Is she a former missionary who learned how to pray effectually and fervently after many years of dedicated ministry? How many years of Sunday school and church services does it take to carve out a woman who is so mighty in prayer? If your back were against the wall, trust me, you would want Silvia Glover in your corner calling out to heaven. But where did this woman come from, and how did she become the prayer warrior she is today?

TRYING TO SURVIVE

Silvia was born in Brooklyn, one of five children, the younger of two sisters. She gravitated toward her father at first and seemed to always be with him—until she was old enough to notice and understand all the different women around him. His growing verbal abuse became a part of her early childhood that was filled with violence. Her father's harsh remarks caused pain that settled deep into Silvia's young heart.

The worsening home situation drove her sister into isolation and silence, but it moved Silvia into the streets. "My mother was forced to work, and no one would be there to supervise us at night," Silvia remembers. "That's when the parties and beer drinking began, even though I was only twelve or thirteen. I went to my first nightclub at age fourteen even though the legal age was twenty-one. With my height, all I needed was a short dress and lots of makeup to get by.

"Even though I could get into the clubs, I felt so alone there and didn't know what to do. My self-esteem was already very low, so I talked only to friends I knew. If a stranger approached, I would clam up and never say a word. I was extremely shy and terrified by the thought of rejection."

But get Silvia filled with alcohol, and she became another person—outgoing, friendly, and risk taking. She soon started smoking marijuana and hanging around low-level drug dealers—street-corner salesmen who were a dime a dozen. She began cutting so many classes that it was a miracle she graduated from high school. Often the police would escort her to school after finding her hanging out in the neighborhood. "Hanging out" had become Silvia's main activity in life.

Now heavily involved in the club scene every night, she made some new friends who were Rastafarians (members of a religious sect origi-nating in Jamaica) and also major drug dealers. Silvia became a Rastafarian at age twenty, which got her more deeply immersed in the drug cul-ture. During Rastafarian religious meetings, she smoked some special marijuana—the best she had ever experienced. The Rastafarians believed that getting high was the way to get closer to God. If that was the case, Silvia and her friends were getting very close to God. Under their influence, she also graduated from marijuana to cocaine and other drugs. She was supplied with whatever she wanted free of charge by a series of boyfriends who were dealing large amounts.

Around this time, Silvia left home. Washington Square Park in lower Manhattan became her new hangout. "Druggies" and criminals, the only people she felt would accept her, became her destructive new family and "support group." She learned to shoplift and became a pro at it. She worked for stores so she could learn how to beat their security systems. She made bogus sales to people and kept the money for herself. When inventory time came around, she moved on to the next scam. She didn't even need the money, though. Her boyfriends gave her everything she needed—some giving her a hundred dollars a day just to take to college—but shoplifting helped her feel more accepted by her new friends.

"Inside I was totally insecure," Silvia recalls. "I had a wall up that kept everyone out. No relationship meant anything to me. No one was ever going to get close to me and hurt me like my father did. I was growing very hard inside, and only alcohol could loosen me up. Only when I drank did I feel free to express myself. Every morning I started with beer, cheap wine, then Hennessy or Absolut. I needed all that to just feel 'right.'

"I was going to college, but my goal was not a college education. I was more interested in having the biggest drug dealer as my boyfriend. I was really crazy because the violence associated with these people was getting ever closer to me. Many of my friends were dead already from drug violence, but I felt it would never reach me. One of my girlfriends was twenty-one and pregnant, but she was with the wrong group at the wrong time. They shot her in the head, then in the belly. Then they murdered her two other children. I was sad, but I couldn't even go to the funeral because that's where bigger shoot-outs occurred between the drug gangs."

Silvia drifted from one boyfriend to another. She dated no one but drug dealers, and some of her boyfriends gave her as much as a thousand dollars a day—for spending money! One boyfriend got violent with her, but she swung at him with her key chain, which had a razor blade connected to it. She broke off that relationship, realizing that if she didn't, someone would soon get hurt.

Silvia's life became a routine of changing schools, jobs, and boyfriends. From Thanksgiving to January of each year, she battled severe depression and even had thoughts of suicide. *Is this all life is about?* She wondered. *Getting high and stealing?* Sin was pulling her out to sea like a deadly undertow. "My life," she says, "became one big scam. I was wanted for shoplifting in a major department store. I stole my father's credit cards and ran up his bill. My new boyfriend was married and had children, but I didn't care. Sometimes his wife would show up at parties, and we'd all be there. It didn't matter. Everyone knew that she was his wife, but I was his girl." About that time, her parents divorced, which brought her to the firm conclusion that marriage doesn't work, so it is better to live together and then move out before you kill each other.

Still, Silvia managed to act as if everything was okay. By hiding her dreadlocks (the hairstyle that is common to Rastafarians) during job interviews, she was able to get jobs that otherwise would have been closed to her. She landed a position in a brokerage firm, which led to involvement in the Wall Street after-hours club scene. To Silvia, it was just more of the same—been there, done that.

"My manager in the brokerage firm was the first Christian I ever met. She was so full of joy that once I asked her, 'What are you smoking, because it's better than what I'm using!' She was a member of the Brooklyn Tabernacle Choir and started praying for me. I was insulted when she repeatedly invited me to church. I thought I could convert her to my lifestyle before she would get to me. Her vice president wondered why she talked with me and befriended such a wild, profane person.

"Then my boyfriend shot someone, and before leaving town for Baltimore to do a drug deal he asked me to ditch the gun. I did as he asked, but he got arrested and was going to do jail time for sure. I was becoming extremely tired of what I called my life. The emptiness inside me seemed to almost cry out, *When will someone love me? When will life mean something?"*

The emptiness inside me seemed to almost cry out, When will someone love me? When will life mean something?

That was the breaking point for Silvia. "I finally agreed to go to church with my manager, although I warned her the building would probably fall down when I stepped inside! God and I did not go together at all—or so I thought. One Sunday I walked into the Brooklyn Tabernacle— a Rastafarian with a turban on my head. I spotted a girl named Pam, who I knew from the club scene. I figured if she could be at church, it couldn't be all that bad. I sat up in the balcony and enjoyed the choir's music, then it was time for the sermon.

"Pastor Cymbala began preaching about the love of God, and soon I was weeping. I knew inside that what he was talking about was what I needed, what I had searched for my whole life. When he offered the invitation to receive Christ, I stood up. My friend who invited me was so shocked she exclaimed, 'What are you doing? Do you know what this means?' I told her, 'Yes, I am going to live for Jesus for the rest of my life.' I walked to the altar, and that was the end of my old life and the beginning of a whole new Silvia Glover."

Silvia quit club hopping, severed ties with drug-dealing boyfriends, and stopped committing crimes. Her countenance was so changed by her inner transformation that friends noticed it immediately. It was evident to everyone that she was a new creation in Jesus Christ. Just as she had served Satan and sin so fervently, Silvia yielded herself wholeheartedly to the things of God. She was willing to do anything and go anywhere for her new Master. Who else but Jesus Christ could embrace such a chaotic life and transform it into a life of virtue and spiritual excellence? I was overwhelmed with thanksgiving when I learned the life story of this prayer warrior who daily holds Carol and me up to God in prayer.

Although Silvia speaks well publicly, her real ministry is that of prayer—as witnessed during those Tuesday nights at the Brooklyn Tabernacle. It is a shame so many churches no longer seek or appreciate this spiritual gifting from God. A heart that prays and a church that gives itself to communion with the Lord—these are two of the great secrets that bring God's blessing in untold ways upon the earth.

A SPECIAL VISIT

Silvia reminds me of Hannah, another woman who had a heart for prayer. The Bible relates that Hannah, like Silvia, lived in a home filled with turmoil. She was one of Elkanah's two wives. Although Hannah was her husband's favorite, this honor was offset by the fact that she could not have children. Making things worse, Elkanah's other wife, Peninnah, had several children and a nasty personality as well. The Bible tells us, "Her rival kept provoking her [Hannah] in order to irritate her" (1 Samuel 1:6). Surely this was a situation that could cause a person to go over the edge.

Every year Hannah would go to the house of the Lord in Shiloh. This was supposed to be a time of praise and thanksgiving for the Israelites, but, accompanied by her unusual and very contentious "extended family," Hannah experienced something quite different. Her rival tormented her even more mercilessly until she wept and was unable even to eat. This went on year after year.

All of Hannah's tears and despair could do nothing to change her life. But one day at Shiloh, Hannah did something that would not only alter her situation but also change the entire course of Israel's history. "Once when they had finished eating and drinking in Shiloh, Hannah stood up" (1 Samuel 1:9). After years of provocation, mocking, and bitterness of soul, Hannah got up and went to the house of God. There she did the only thing that could turn her life around. "Hannah wept much and *prayed to the LORD*" (v. 10). She had shed many tears of self-pity before, but now something else was going on. She poured out her soul to the Lord. She laid before him her dilemma and the opposition she faced.

This was not the kind of praying we often hear or practice ourselves. "Hannah was *pray-*

ing in her heart" (v. 13), and therein lies the difference. Her prayer was not a tidy little product of her mind alone. It was far more than that. It was a gushing out to God of all that was in her beleaguered heart. And when any needy heart begins to truly pray, heaven itself stirs in response to the cry for help. Hannah's story is not about melodrama or emotional fanaticism. It is inspired Scripture that teaches us the power of a heart that pleads its case before the Lord.

When any needy heart begins to truly pray, heaven itself stirs in response.

When Hannah poured out her soul, she tapped into the resources of the Almighty. Until that moment, there is no record that she had the faith to ask God to change her situation. But as she stood and went to pray that day in Shiloh, her life was changed forever.

In response to Hannah's earnest prayer of the heart, God gave her a son, whom she named Samuel. Because she knew that this son came from God in answer to her prayer, she dedicated him for service in the temple. That little boy grew up worshiping in the house of the Lord and later became a great prophet in the land of Israel. His spiritual influence stands in sharp contrast to the dark days recorded in the book of Judges when "everyone did as he saw fit" (Judges 21:25).

God used Samuel to alter the history of a whole nation (1 Samuel 4:1), but that should be no surprise. Samuel was not only a product of Hannah and her husband; he was a product of heaven's response to a heart that poured itself out to the Lord in prayer. (By the way, God blessed Hannah with five more children after the birth of Samuel!)

BARREN LIVES, WITHERED CHURCHES

Eli, the priest in charge of the house of God at Shiloh, symbolized the sad state of spiritual affairs in Israel. He was so backslidden that he mistook Hannah's silent yet intense praying as a sign that she was drunk! How similar this is to the religious establishment today. Many church leaders schedule almost every kind of church function other than a prayer meeting. They tolerate anything but a fervent outpouring of someone's heart to God during a service. They want everything to be neat, organized, and programmed to the minute. It is frightening that so few churches today take God seriously when he declares that his house should be called a house of prayer (Isaiah 56:7; Matthew 21:13). God wants to remind us that *nothing* on earth or in hell can ultimately stand against the man or the woman who calls on the name of the Lord!

After I wrote my first book, *Fresh Wind, Fresh Fire*, I was stunned by one of the criticisms leveled at me. A religious leader dismissed our Tuesday night prayer meeting and the ministry of people like Silvia Glover as having nothing to do with God's blessings on our church or his answers to our prayer requests. His approach was, "How can mere men affect a sovereign God? How can frail, human prayers move the hand of the Creator of the universe? God is going to do what he pleases, so forget about linking God's activity with the prayers of people." God wants to remind us that *nothing* on earth or in hell can ultimately stand against the man or the woman who calls on the name of the Lord!

No wonder there are so many spiritually barren lives and withered churches throughout our nation and the world! If these assertions are true, we had better throw out our Bibles, for the Scriptures continually encourage us to open our hearts to God in real prayer so that he can answer us and provide the blessings we desperately need. He promises, "Call upon me in the day of trouble; I will deliver you, and you will honor me" (Psalm 50:15). King David was faced with all kinds of opposition and problems, but this one thing he knew: "*I call* to the LORD, who is worthy of praise, and *I am saved* from my enemies" (2 Samuel 22:4). David trusted that "the LORD will hear *when* I call to him" (Psalm 4:3) and proclaimed that "in the day of my trouble I will call to you [God], for *you will answer* me" (Psalm 86:7).

But if we do not have hearts that call out to him, we forfeit the deliverance. "You do not have, because you do not ask God" (James 4:2) is probably the saddest possible commentary on any life—especially the life of a Christian. Imagine the tragedy of God wanting to do things to help and strengthen us but being constrained by *his own law* of asking and receiving.

I believe it is wiser for us to build our lives on the sure Word of God and David's firsthand experience than on a theology of cynicism and unbelief.

LISTEN TO THE STIRRINGS OF YOUR HEART

Are you going through a season of trouble right now? Have you, like Hannah, tried everything except praying to God—and found only confusion and despair? What would happen if you were to turn your heart toward heaven and lay everything that is in it before the Lord? You don't need fancy words or religious phrases. Just tell God the way it really is. Let your heart do the talking. Your situation might not be like that of Silvia Glover, but God answered her simple prayer for deliverance—so what will he do for you?

You don't need fancy words or religious phrases. Just tell God the way it really is.

There is one more question I'd like to ask. As you read about Silvia, did you feel the stirrings of the Spirit within your soul? Possibly the ministry of prayer God has given her is the very thing you have felt called to do. You may not be a pastor, teacher, or gifted musician, but the thought of interceding for people in need creates a holy excitement within you.

You may have run from this calling or neglected it for years. But today can be a turning point in your life. Forget the failures of the past, and give your heart over to prayer so that the Lord can use you to bring blessings to others in ways you could never imagine. If God could use heartbroken Hannah to change a nation, what will he do through you? And if a wild and hardened heart like Silvia's could be transformed into a modern Hannah, then no excuse should hold us back from God's best for our lives.

This very moment his ear is open to the cry of your heart.

Lord, we bring our burdens and heartaches to you at the throne of grace. You have promised to help us in our time of trouble and need. We rest upon your Word and cast every one of these cares upon you. Work on our behalf so that others might know the awesomeness of your power and the faithfulness of your love. In Christ's name, amen.

FIVE

THE POWER OF
TENDERNESS

During my sophomore year at the University of Rhode Island, I started for the varsity basketball team. We had some talented players and made a strong showing early in our twenty-six-game schedule.

In mid-December we were scheduled to play rare, back-to-back home games on consecutive nights in Keaney Gymnasium on our beautiful campus in Kingston, Rhode Island.

The first night we beat St. John's University. I was delighted to have two close friends, Wayne and Richard, visiting me from New York City. They cheered wildly for both the team and me as we came out on top in a real dogfight of a game. The next night our opponent was Brown University, an Ivy League school also located in Rhode Island. We expected this game to be much easier than the previous one.

My friends and I left my dormitory early so I would have plenty of time to get taped and dressed for the game. It was snowing lightly as we piled into Richard's 1963 VW bug and headed up the steep road that bordered my dormitory. The car about one hundred feet in front of us stopped, as expected, at the corner stop sign. Then it suddenly started accelerating toward us in reverse. It was heading straight for us! Even in perfect weather Richard could never have gotten us out of the way. I ducked and braced myself in the backseat when I saw the collision coming.

The out-of-control car's back end blasted into us with tremendous force. Glass flew everywhere. The force of the impact sent the front seats back against my shins with such force that I still bear a small dent in the shinbone of my left leg.

I was fortunate compared to Wayne, who was sitting on the passenger side. Shattered glass had showered him, and blood was running down his face. All three of us pried ourselves out of the now-totaled VW and struggled toward the car that had collided with us. I got there first and opened the driver's side door. What I saw didn't help my already stunned state.

The middle-aged driver was slumped over the wheel, motionless. Next to him, a female student in an obvious state of shock looked straight ahead with a glassy stare. She didn't respond to me at all, even though I tried to talk with her and find out what we could do for her. Then, without thinking about proper medical procedures, I tried to lift the driver out of the car. As I wrapped my arms around his shoulders and neck, he gurgled and then fell against me. He literally died in my arms.

The student never looked at me or said a word the whole time I was with her. I learned later that the driver was her father and he was taking her home for the Christmas break. He had suffered a heart attack at the stop sign. As he fell forward, he simultaneously knocked the car into reverse and hit the gas pedal with his foot.

Students came running toward the accident and told me they would get the campus police, so I turned my attention to my friends. Wayne had a face full of blood; Richard was doing somewhat better. Someone yelled for us to take Wayne to the campus infirmary, which was less than a hundred yards away. As we hurried through the snow, someone gave Wayne a cloth to wipe his bloodied face. Richard had some lacerations, and I was limping slightly from the bruise I had received at impact. The three of us together must have been quite a sight.

The campus infirmary at URI in the mid-sixties was not exactly a state-of-the-art emergency room or trauma center. In fact, only a young student nurse was on duty that evening; the regular nurse had left for the day. I will never forget the student nurse's first reaction when we stumbled through the door. We were all slightly spaced-out from the impact of the accident; Wayne's blood was everywhere—including on Richard and me. When the student nurse looked up to see what the commotion was all about, she let out a high-pitched scream that let us know we were not exactly dealing with a seasoned, trauma-experienced Florence Nightingale. She looked panicked. For a second I thought she might need some medical care herself. Thank God, she calmed down and took control of the situation. She examined each of us in turn, starting with Wayne, and patched up our cuts. We could hear the sirens blaring as an ambulance whisked the man and his daughter to a nearby hospital.

Emotionally drained and bruised, I answered a police officer's questions before finally returning to my dormitory to change clothes. I managed to get to the field house just before game time, but I wasn't much use to the team that night. I did the best I could despite the weird numbness that affected me mentally, emotionally, and physically. I kept thinking about the father and his daughter. Tears almost came to my eyes several times. I kept picturing the man's face after he died . . . the girl's glazed eyes. . . . But I had to focus my thoughts and emotions on basketball.

We won the game, and Richard, Wayne, and I eventually healed and went on with our lives. It was definitely a night to remember—or maybe to forget—in Kingston, Rhode Island. I had suddenly been confronted with death . . . and the opportunity to try to help the badly shaken daughter. The emotional student nurse, too, had been confronted with a situation in which people needed emergency care. Fortunately, she responded professionally to each of us as best she could after the initial shock wore off.

How we respond to people and events,

especially during a crisis, reveals a lot

about who we really are.

As this story illustrates, how you and I respond to people and events, especially during a crisis, reveals a lot about who we really are. And nowhere is this more true than in our relationship with God. Although a sensitive heart makes us vulnerable in other aspects of life, it is essential and leads to great blessing when we're dealing with the Lord. In fact, the cold, mechanical professionalism that is admired in many fields of work will actually lead us into trouble in the realm of spiritual living. The Scriptures are filled with warnings about a callous, insensitive, and hard heart toward the Lord. We are never to stop *feeling* things as we serve Christ. In fact, our tenderness in response to things like God's love, our own sin, and the needs of others will become more acute as we grow closer to the Lord. This is one of the signs of a devoted, godly life.

TURNING THE TIDE

If I had my way, next to the word *tender* in a Bible dictionary there would be a picture of King Josiah. He was only an eight-year-old boy when he ascended to the throne of Judah in place of his wicked father, Amon. During the reigns of Josiah's father and his grandfather, Manasseh, the nation had experienced more than a half century of nearly unbroken ungodliness from the royal throne. Instead of reigning in righteousness, these two kings followed every detestable practice of the pagan nations God had driven out of the land. The throne of Judah led the people astray. Evidence of idolatry and immorality was everywhere. Baal altars and Asherah poles dotted Jerusalem, and Jehovah's chosen people made sacrifices to these abominations. Even children were offered in the fire as living sacrifices. Sorcery, divination, and witchcraft were practiced by the kings and common people alike. Not even the temple built by Solomon was untouched. It was profaned by an idolatrous, carved image and all sorts of other blasphemy.

This moral and spiritual swamp was the setting in which Josiah was placed as ruler at the tender age of eight. To human eyes, it probably appeared that there was no hope for spiritual reformation; the nation was only enduring a waiting period before God's judgment would fall. Scripture, however, reveals that something quite unusual occurred, something totally unexpected:

> In the *eighth year* of his reign, while he [Josiah] was still young, he began to seek the God of his father David. In his *twelfth year* he began to purge Judah and Jerusalem of high places, Asherah poles, carved idols and cast images. Under his direction the altars of the Baals were torn down; he cut to pieces the incense altars that were above them, and smashed the Asherah poles, the

idols and the images. These he broke to pieces and scattered over the graves of those who had sacrificed to them. He burned the bones of the priests on their altars, and so he purged Judah and Jerusalem (2 Chronicles 34:3—5).

What happened? Surrounded by idolatry and a corrupt religious establishment, sixteen-year-old Josiah went against the evil tide swirling around him and the nation—everything he had ever known—and began "to seek the God of his father David." King David had been dead for hundreds of years, but Josiah somehow yearned for the spiritual paths of the king who had a heart after God's own heart. Was it Josiah's conscience that inspired his yearning for God? Was it the still, small voice of the Spirit or the voice of one of the Hebrew prophets that stirred Josiah's heart? We don't know for sure, but for some reason the teenage king started on a spiritual pilgrimage that would affect the entire nation of Judah.

After seeking God for four years, twenty-year-old Josiah became sensitive to the abominable idolatry that permeated Judah and took far-reaching

action. During the next few years, he ranged far
and wide in a search-and-destroy mode. Everything associated with pagan worship was disman-
tled and destroyed. He had such earnestness of
conviction that he even ventured into the northern tribes of Israel, zealously ridding the land of
the idolatry that had polluted it for so long.

At age twenty-six Josiah focused his attention on other things that troubled his spiritually
sensitive heart. Although much had been done,
the temple of Jehovah was still in disrepair. The
people had not celebrated proper religious obser-
vances there for years. So King Josiah sent a crew
to repair the temple and ordered the Levites to
collect funds to finance the extensive, much-
needed renovation of God's house.

We can only imagine the bustling activities—
laborers moving rocks and rubbish, carpenters saw-
ing timbers that would be used for joists, Levite
supervisors calling out orders, supply carts wind-
ing their way up the road, scribes taking inventory.

THE DISCOVERY

While the rebuilding was going on, "Hilkiah the
priest found the Book of the Law of the LORD that

had been given through Moses" (2 Chronicles 34:14). He gave the Scriptures to Shaphan, the secretary, who read them to the king.

This is hard to believe! Josiah, king of Judah, was in his mid-twenties before he even heard anyone read the Book of the Law! The Scriptures probably had been lost in the neglected temple for decades. Up to this point in his life, all of King Josiah's seeking after God had been done without the benefit of the Holy Scriptures given through Moses.

As we look closer at this story, we discover that Shaphan was so unaware of the significance of the Book of the Law that he didn't even mention it until after he reported to King Josiah on the progress of the temple's renovation. Only then did he add, "Hilkiah the priest has given me *a book*" (v. 18). Notice that he said "a book" as if he were holding some old volume that was extremely overdue at the Jerusalem Library. The king, however, had quite a different response to that old book.

Josiah's tender heart was cut to the quick when the Law of the Lord was read to him. "When the king heard the words of the Law, he tore his robes. . . . 'Go and inquire of the LORD for

me and for the remnant in Israel and Judah about
what is written in this book that has been found.
Great is the LORD's anger that is poured out on us
because our fathers have not kept the word of the
LORD; they have not acted in accordance with all
that is written in this book'" (vv. 19, 21).

---

*For the first time Josiah realized all the
promises that had been forfeited because
of spiritual infidelity.*

Josiah had followed all the limited spiritual
light that he had up to this moment. But now,
like a tremendous blast of pure sunlight invad-
ing a pitch-black room, the truths of God entered
his mind and soul. For the first time the king
understood the full extent of the evil that had
taken place—all the trampling of God's commands that had gone on for decades. For the first
time he realized all the promises that had been
forfeited because of spiritual infidelity. For the

first time he saw divine judgment hanging like a sword over a people who had turned their backs on Jehovah innumerable times. He now felt that he needed a word from the Lord regarding what he should do at this critical moment.

PROPHETIC WORDS

Immediately obeying the king's order, the officials sought out a prophetess named Huldah who lived in Jerusalem. Her prophetic response contains a truth that is vital for our own spiritual progress:

> Thus says the LORD, the God of Israel, "Tell the man who sent you to Me, . . . 'Behold, I am bringing evil [disaster] on this place and on its inhabitants. . . . Because they have forsaken Me and have burned incense to other gods, that they might provoke Me to anger with all the works of their hands; therefore My wrath will be poured out on this place, and it shall not be quenched.' But to the king of Judah who sent you to inquire of the LORD, thus you will say to him, . . .

'Because *your heart was tender* and you humbled yourself before God . . . and wept before Me, I truly have heard you,' declares the LORD. 'Behold, I will gather you to your fathers and you shall be gathered to your grave in peace, so your eyes shall not see all the evil which I will bring on this place and on its inhabitants'" (2 Chronicles 34:23–28 NASB).

It was too late for Judah to escape God's righteous judgment, but it wasn't too late for Josiah, the man with the spiritually tender heart.

Think about these words: "Because your heart was tender and you humbled yourself before God." The word translated "tender" means "soft and responsive." Josiah was so sensitive to the newly discovered Book of the Law that its truths struck his soul like arrows. He humbled himself and shed tears because of the grief his people had caused God for so many decades. He could have justified himself because of his exemplary spiritual leadership. He could have blamed his forefathers and the people for the horrible plight of the nation. But then Josiah wouldn't have been such a treasure to God.

The king's tender heart meant so much to God that he postponed judgment until Josiah was lying peacefully in his grave. Josiah's *heart-felt response* to the Lord and his Word brought joy to the God of heaven. Judah had suffered much under the rule of hard-hearted leaders, but finally God had found a heart that was tender and sensitive to his touch.

Josiah began his extraordinary reign by seeking the God of his spiritually minded ancestor, David. And it was this same David who gives us great insight into just how much the Lord values a certain kind of heart: "The LORD is close to the *brokenhearted* and saves those who are crushed in spirit" (Psalm 34:18). And again: "The sacrifices of God are a *broken* spirit; a *broken and contrite heart*, O God, you will not despise" (Psalm 51:17).

Josiah offered up a far better sacrifice than anything burnt on the altar in the temple, and he was saved from judgment. His responsiveness— his deep sensitivity—to what God said and felt made him one of the greatest of all who sat on the throne in Jerusalem. Through his leadership, which flowed from his tender heart, he so power-fully impacted his nation that "as long as he lived, they [the people] did not fail to follow the LORD, the God of their fathers" (2 Chronicles 34:33). Just think: because of one man's respon-sive heart, not only he but an entire nation received blessing and a temporary stay of judg-ment. Look at the effect his simple, childlike, and tender heart had on God!

Because of one man's responsive heart,

both he and an entire nation received

blessing and a stay of judgment.

FULL OF RELIGION

Now fast-forward with me through time to a syn-agogue in Israel more than six hundred years after Josiah's reign, to the day the Pharisees first plot-ted to destroy Jesus. In Mark 3:1–6 the story is told of Jesus' healing of a man with a shriveled hand. The Pharisees were watching closely. The reason for their intense scrutiny reveals much about their hearts. Their interest was not in the man who was suffering with a physical handicap. They cared nothing about him. No, they were watching to see if Jesus would heal a withered hand and in so doing break their rules about "working" on the Sabbath! Having placed so many interpretations and traditions upon the commands of God, the Pharisees ended up setting aside the very Scriptures they quoted. They had hardened their hearts against the Word of God. Before he healed, "Jesus asked them, 'Which is lawful on the Sabbath: to do good or to do evil, to save life or to kill?' But they remained silent" (v. 4).

Such a simple question should have an obvious answer, right? Well, no. Not if you are filled with religious tradition up to your eyeballs. Not if you have lips that honor God but a heart that is light-years away from feeling his love and mercy. It is important to remember that the Pharisees who refused to answer Jesus that day were not secular humanists or liberal theologians. In fact, they were the Bible-thumping fundamentalists of their day. The Pharisees believed that *all* Old Testament

Scripture was inspired by God. They were the ultraconservatives who believed in angels, spirits, and the resurrection of the dead. They would have argued until 4:00 A.M. that God literally opened up the Red Sea and that God enabled Elijah to raise the widow's child from the dead.

The Pharisees could quote the Scriptures by memory, yet didn't recognize the Son of the living God—the Messiah of Israel—standing ten feet in front of them! They were full of religion, but they knew nothing of God and his heart.

Their stubborn silence drew a strong response from Jesus: "After looking around at them with *anger*, grieved at their *hardness of heart* . . ." (Mark 3:5 NASB). Jesus didn't get angry often, but this was one time he did. What incensed him was the *hardness of heart* he saw among the religious leaders of Israel. They made a mockery of serving God and kept people out of his kingdom rather than leading them into it. It was they who were the "shriveled" ones in the synagogue that day. The poor man had a problem with one hand, but the religious leaders were suffering from withered hearts! And Jesus was not only angry, he was also grieved. How sad it is when "religious" folk become callous in their hearts by years of traditionalism and mechanical service.

What does this have to do with you and me? Everything! We had better quickly discover whether we have mere religion or a real experience with Jesus, whether we have outward observance of religious forms or hearts that beat in tune with God. We can go to church every Sunday and quote the Bible but still not have a clue about what is really important to God. We can more easily drift into being a mere Baptist, charismatic, or Presbtyerian evangelical than being a tenderhearted, Spirit-filled follower of the Savior. I meet many people who know more about their denominational traditions than they know about God. This is a danger for all of us.

We must never forget that it was religious folks with hard hearts who put Jesus on the cross. Instead of rejoicing after Jesus healed the man's hand, "the Pharisees went out and began to plot with the Herodians how they might kill Jesus" (Mark 3:6). They were too busy plotting the murder of Jesus Christ to even think about rejoicing in what God had done. If this doesn't cause us to search ourselves, I don't know what will.

How many churches today resemble that synagogue where Jesus taught?

How many churches today resemble that synagogue where Jesus taught—where there is lots of judging and condemning but little manifestation of God's tender heart, where people know Scripture but have no sensitivity to divine love and compassion, where traditions are followed scrupulously but little attention is given to the hurting among us? The Pharisees of Jesus' day were upset by the thought of Sabbath violations, but then planned the destruction of Israel's Messiah on the very same day. How blind tradition can make us! How hard the human heart can be even though it is religious to the core!

Perhaps now we can better understand why Jehovah was delighted by King Josiah's tender heart and tears. He was already anticipating the terrible days ahead when his Son would be rejected by religious hearts as hard as stone. The Pharisees had the Scriptures given by God through Moses, but the Scriptures didn't do the religious leaders any good. King Josiah, in contrast, discovered the Word of God and took every word of it to heart.

Let us follow Josiah's example so we can continually offer God the sacrifice of a broken, contrite, and tender heart. This is what the Lord desires more than any outward observance of religious ritual and tradition. This kind of tender sensitivity to him not only brings joy to his heart, but prepares us to be a great blessing to others who need his love. Even as Josiah turned a whole nation back toward God, we will find that our own tenderness of heart will lead to wonderful, new experiences in God.

"Then I will teach transgressors your ways, and sinners will turn back to you" (Psalm 51:13).

Lord, *strip away the layers of hardness and religious traditionalism that have accumulated through the years. Make us like little children who have tender and teachable hearts. Give us a new sensitivity to your Word and an openness to your will concerning our lives. In Christ's name, amen.*

SIX

The Last
Half Hour

When my wife and I came to the Brooklyn Tabernacle in 1972, it was a struggling little church.* Only a handful of people attended. The church's checking account had less than ten dollars in it—an usher had been stealing from the offering plate for months. The run-down building on Atlantic Avenue was depressing, inside and outside. The little sanctuary had broken-down pews. The sanctuary ceiling had a large sag in it and eventually collapsed completely at the

---

*I have written about some of these challenges in my first book, *Fresh Wind, Fresh Fire.*

end of one Sunday service. The neighborhood was filled with poverty and drugs. Hookers plied their trade less than two blocks away. There wasn't much to be encouraged about.

Carol was a preacher's kid by birth and an excellent musician by gifting from God, so she had a head start in the ministry. It was much harder for me to find my niche. The early going in Brooklyn was slow and difficult, but eventually I began to see some light at the end of the tunnel. As I studied my Bible and spent time in prayer, I felt assured that God had called us to the ministry and had sovereignly placed us right where we were.

Despite the seemingly insurmountable challenges, God had plans for us in that church and in the community.

Gradually, as I sought the Lord, a number of promises from his Word came alive. In my heart, as I began to rely upon them in prayer, God dis-

pelled my sense of being overwhelmed. The Holy
Spirit was helping me to understand the truths of
Scripture, which in turn gave me the faith to trust
the Lord. Despite the bleak surroundings and
seemingly insurmountable challenges, God had
plans for us in that church and in the community.
Why would he have put us in downtown Brooklyn except to use us to reach people and bring
glory to his name? We didn't have to merely tread
water and try to survive. Why couldn't the Lord
show himself powerful in our situation—just as
he had done in the book of Acts? For example:

> Those who accepted his message were bap-
> tized, and about three thousand were
> added to their number that day (Acts 2:41).

> Every day they continued to meet together
> in the temple courts. They broke bread in
> their homes and ate together with glad and
> sincere hearts, praising God and enjoying
> the favor of all the people. And the Lord
> added to their number daily those who
> were being saved (Acts 2:46–47).

> Now those who had been scattered by the
> persecution in connection with Stephen

traveled as far as Phoenicia, Cyprus and Antioch. . . . The Lord's hand was with them, and a great number of people believed and turned to the Lord (Acts 11:19, 21).

PRAYER IS VITAL

I also came to realize more and more that prayer was the key. After all, God was the only One who could take an untrained, inexperienced person like me and make me effective in ministry. Who else but the Lord could help Carol and me see unbelievers transformed through the preaching of the gospel in the power of the Spirit? One Sunday, with all these convictions in mind, I invited anyone who might be available to join me for a special, midmorning prayer time the following Thursday.

When the day arrived, a group of six or seven gathered with me in a room on the second floor of the church. We knelt and began to pour out our hearts to God. A few led out in prayer, and I pleaded with God to help me overcome all the negative thoughts that often attacked my mind. We had a real breakthrough as we prayed that morning. God lifted our hearts, and we just *knew* things would turn around soon. I got up from my knees with fresh inspiration and a stronger desire to serve the Lord.

After everyone left, I was alone in my "office." (It measured about seven by seven feet!) The phone rang immediately, which was unusual. I didn't need a switchboard operator in those days because no one ever called the little church that had big problems. I said, "Hello," and a woman's shrill voice ran right through my "Who's calling, please?" It was a tirade right from the get-go, but I didn't know who it was or why she was calling.

"Listen, you little white devil!" she exclaimed. "Who do you think you're fooling? You and your ugly white face down there with all those blacks and Puerto Ricans." I tried to interrupt, but she was on a roll. I slowly sat down behind my desk.

"I know you, you understand? You're nothing but a devil like the rest of them."

"But, but, but . . . wait," I stammered, trying to say something to stop her.

"Shut up, you cracker. You're a joke; your church is a joke. Get it?"

"But I'm not like that!" I yelled out.

"I said shut up, didn't I? I'm making this call, and I know you're nothing but a phony white devil."

She went on and on and on. I stood up as in protest, but I finally gave up trying to talk. I could feel my heart pounding. Tears welled up in my eyes.

"So, you remember," she continued. "I know what you really are! Get it? You're a good-for-nothing white devil! Okay, I've got to go now. God bless!" Then she hung up!

I don't know how long I continued to stand with the receiver at my ear. I was absolutely stunned and emotionally devastated. She had never let me say one thing in defense or explanation!

I grew up around prejudice against minorities and witnessed some horrific examples of it in prep school and college. But playing basketball on the city playgrounds had helped educate me—even more than anything I heard or saw in church. I had learned that everybody is the same inside, that the outside differences of color are irrelevant when it comes to discovering who people really are. I knew areas of my life were not Christlike, but that woman's angry, racist accusations hurt and frustrated me because they were so false.

I finally dropped into my chair and exploded into tears as my head fell onto the desk. My mind raced, full of questions. *What was that call all about? What have I done to deserve such an attack? Who was she? Did she visit our church? No, that couldn't be—no one visits our church! We are lucky if the few members show up.*

Then it hit me. *Wait a minute! We were just calling on God in prayer. Is this some kind of answer? If so, I'd better stop praying immediately. I don't need any more answers like that!*

CLINGING TO GOD'S PROMISES

I had gone to God in prayer because I thought he was going to turn our dismal situation around. I had believed in his promise that he would send mercy and grace "to help us during our time of need" (Hebrews 4:16). But now I was wondering, *Where are his mercy and grace? How will things ever turn around if crazy people like that woman start calling me?*

A battle within me had begun. The spiritual lines were drawn. I had to choose between what I knew in my heart God had promised to do and the negative situations I saw with my eyes and felt with my heart every day. This struggle to fight for what God has promised rather than surrendering to what can be seen and felt has continued through all the years Carol and I have served the Lord at the Brooklyn Tabernacle. God has continually led us to trust in him for greater things, but there is an ever-present tension between the greatness of his promises and the still-unchanged situations we face after we pray.

There is an ever-present tension between the greatness of God's promises and the still-unchanged situations we face after we pray.

This problem is not peculiar to Carol and me. Throughout history men and women who trusted the Lord have had to learn the importance of "the last half hour." It is one of the lessons we can learn from a fascinating passage in Isaiah. Although this prophetic chapter deals primarily with the promised Messiah, it contains a spiritual secret we need to understand today.

Note the promise in Isaiah 49:8: "This is what the LORD says: 'In the time of my favor I will answer you, and in the day of salvation I will help you.'" Isn't this a wonderful promise? In no uncertain terms, God affirms the fact that he *will answer* and *will help* his people. But notice carefully the time slot for his help and answers: "In the time of my favor ... and in the day of salvation." God has a designated time when his promise will be fulfilled and the prayer will be answered. It is a "day" or moment that he knows is best for the help to arrive and the deliverance to be accomplished. His answer is *absolutely sure* for those who trust him, but it is *not yet*.

Herein lies the battle of faith—to hold on and keep believing God despite what our natural senses tell us. Our challenge is to *wait in faith* for the day of God's favor and salvation.

How many times have we battled this seeming contradiction? We are stirred to the core by God's promises, or we hear a sermon that focuses on a need in our lives. We know the Lord's record of faithfulness to countless generations. We pray with all our hearts and take our stand on his

Word. But then . . . nothing, absolutely nothing, seems to change. No miraculous supply comes within twenty-four hours; no dramatic change occurs in our difficult family situation. In fact, sometimes our circumstances seem to *worsen!* The wayward child we interceded for and claimed for Christ becomes more, not less, rebellious. The finances don't increase, but new bills arrive in the mail or we get laid off from our jobs.

God knows our tendency to give up during these seeming times of silence from heaven: "But Zion said, 'The LORD has forsaken me, the Lord has forgotten me'" (Isaiah 49:14). Because the people of God back in Isaiah's day didn't see the fulfillment of the divine promise, they felt abandoned. "Where is God in all this?" they asked. "How can his promise be true? He must have forgotten us or forsaken us because of our past sins." God, who is always grieved when his people fail to trust him, responded immediately: "Can a mother forget the baby at her breast and have no compassion on the child she has borne? Though *she* may forget, *I will not forget you!* See, I have engraved you on the palms of my hands; your walls are ever before me" (vv. 15–16).

Can a normal mother forget or lose interest in the infant she nursed, the child she bore? Won't her heart always be knit to the offspring of her body? How much more does our loving Father cherish you and me? After giving his Son on Calvary as a sacrifice for *our* sins, will God now abandon us? Will he let his beloved children fall into some kind of "black hole"? Is it conceivable that he will forget us when the Lamb of God is seated in heaven with those nail prints still in his hands?

Whatever the words meant to the people in Isaiah's day, we should shout with joy when we read, "I have engraved you on the palms of my hands." It was done on Calvary! The resurrected Christ appeared to his disciples with the wounds still in his hands! No matter which difficulties we face or how badly life seems to be going, we must cling to God's unchanging promise that has comforted millions down through the ages: "I will not forget you!" We need not be discouraged by what we "see" or distracted by how we feel emotionally. This truth is forever settled in heaven: "I will not forget you!" And God can do anything but lie!

WAITING ISN'T EASY

This assurance of God's concern and faithfulness expressed in Isaiah 49 is a great encouragement to our faith, but the hardest element of faith is waiting for that "time of favor" to come, isn't it? It is during the waiting that discouragement often sets in. It is also the time when Satan slanders God and puts powerful temptations before us. There is danger when we look away from the promise and who made it. We often give in to panic and the urge to take matters into our own feeble hands. The glow of fresh faith fades away as the days, weeks, months, and sometimes even years go by without seeing our prayers answered. *Will things ever change?* we wonder. *Is it worth it to keep on trying to believe?*

These are real questions that every real follower of God has dealt with sometime in life. That's why one of my favorite portions of Scripture is a passage from another part of Isaiah's prophecy:

Why do you say, O Jacob, and complain,
O Israel, "My way is hidden from the
LORD; my cause is disregarded by my

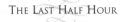

God"? Do you not know? Have you not heard? The LORD is the everlasting God, the Creator of the ends of the earth. He will not grow tired or weary, and his understanding no one can fathom (Isaiah 40:27–28).

Our difficult situations are not hidden from God, nor are we being disregarded because we don't yet see the answer. Furthermore, we don't have to give in to unbelief because God gives "power to the weak."

And to those who have no might He increases strength. Even the youths shall faint and be weary, And the young men shall utterly fall, But those who *wait on the LORD* Shall renew *their* strength; They shall mount up with wings like eagles, They shall run and not be weary, They shall walk and not faint (vv. 29–31 NKJV).

The secret is to have a heart that *waits on the Lord*, to keep waiting in faith and glad expectation for the things he has promised.

The secret is to have a heart that waits on the Lord.

The challenge before us is to have faith in God, and the hardest part of faith is the *waiting*. And the hardest part of waiting is the last half hour. We start by believing and praying, but we need to go further by waiting until that promised moment when God will visit us with grace and power. What a tragedy it is when we give up short of the goal line—that "time of favor" and "day of salvation" when God will respond as promised.

Jesus laid down as a first principle, "According to your faith will it be done to you" (Matthew 9:29). But to receive the blessing we need, we must believe and keep on believing, to wait and keep on waiting. We need to *wait* in prayer, *wait* with our Bibles open as we confess his promises, *wait* in joyful praise and worship of the God who will never forget our case, and *wait* as we continue serving others in his name.

No wonder David gives us so many encouragements to keep on waiting in faith! Listen:

> Indeed, let no one who *waits* on You be ashamed;. . . For You *are* the God of my salvation; On You I *wait* all the day (Psalm 25:3, 5 NKJV).

> *Wait* on the LORD; Be of good courage, And He shall strengthen your heart; *Wait,* I say, on the LORD! (Psalm 27:14 NKJV).

> I *waited* patiently for the LORD; And He inclined to me, And heard my cry (Psalm 40:1 NKJV).

Most of us know that "without faith it is impossible to please God" (Hebrews 11:6), yet many of us don't realize that the same is true about waiting on the Lord. Having faith and waiting on the Lord are part of the same package. I have been aware of this truth for many years, but I am always discovering new lessons. I am blessed over and over again when I see God unfolding his plans as his people wait in faith with open hearts to receive from him.

LESSONS IN THE SCHOOL OF FAITH

As I write this book, for example, the Brooklyn Tabernacle faces a new challenge that is forcing us to trust God in a greater dimension than ever before. As the senior pastor, I have had to take some more advanced classes in the School of Faith. Motivated by God's promptings and four over-crowded services every Sunday, the leadership of our congregation began looking for a new church campus. After much prayer and diligent search-ing, we found a four-thousand-seat theater that was built in 1918 and is located in the heart of downtown Brooklyn. We purchased it, along with two connected buildings, even though we had no money when negotiations began. God provided in incredible ways, but the purchase only drew us into deeper waters. The scope of the renovation was tremendous and would entail complicated and costly restructuring to meet our needs as a church. In addition, all of the buildings were in terrible disrepair. Magnificent plasterwork on the vast ceilings had been destroyed by water dam-age. Between New York City construction costs and architectural fees, new mechanical systems, façades, roofing, and many other details, the renovation budget called for millions of dollars! That's a huge sum of money for any organization, but especially an inner-city church.

Although the situation did not look favorable, the Lord continued to help us. Large, unsolicited gifts came in along with the regular giving of both the congregation and friends around the country. A Christian organization also approached us and offered to lend us money. After seeking God's leading, we accepted the loan so that construction could proceed as quickly as possible. After all, the new facility would give us the potential of reaching up to twelve thousand people in just three services each Sunday. It would also provide more space for children's programs, youth outreach, discipling classes, and major evangelistic efforts. Plans were drawn up and filed with the city building department, and the long renovation process began. The first order of business was a huge demolition job to remove old systems and furnishings.

BURDENED BY FEAR

As the demolition stage was ending, I went to South America with Carol and a small missions team from the Brooklyn Tabernacle. There we ministered to hundreds of pastors, some of whom lived in impoverished conditions and had traveled long distances to be with us. We also gave out hundreds of complimentary copies of my book in Spanish. Although it may seem strange for a church that still didn't know how it would complete the new campus project to be spending thousands of dollars on missions work, we paid for all our travel expenses and also helped feed the pastors who attended the conference.

Just before I left for that trip, I had received a call from the organization that was lending us money. An official pointed out that they had carefully reviewed our "phase one" costs. Even with their loan, he informed me, there was a six-million-dollar shortfall. He asked how we planned to meet it and get the work completed so that we could begin services at the new site. I had no answer, but reminded him that when they approached us and offered to help, we had made it clear that we were walking by faith. I assured him that we would continue praying as a church and would believe God for the needed funds.

While I was in South America, that six-million-dollar figure started to get my attention.

Where will we get that kind of money? I wondered.
It certainly can't come from our congregation alone.
We don't have that kind of economic base. Then the
fearful questions began. *What if we run short and*
the work has to stop? What am I doing to raise this
money? What should I be doing?

I know of only two ways to raise large sums
of money: pray and give. Jesus said, "Ask and it
will be given to you" (Matthew 7:7). The Lord
has promised to answer when we lay our needs
before him. Jesus also promised, "Give, and it
will be given to you" (Luke 6:38). So I pondered
our situation. I reminded the Lord that we as a
church had been praying regularly and fervently
about this project. We were also giving faithfully
to several kingdom causes, including our present
labor in South America. Even so, that phone call
and the six-million-dollar shortfall lay heavily on
my mind and heart.

One afternoon I took a walk to pray. Instead
of focusing on God, however, I began thinking
of all the appeal letters I should probably be
writing. Maybe a phone call to someone with big
bucks was the answer. Did I know anyone with
that kind of money? As I churned inside, I

sensed God speaking to my heart. "Leave it with me," he seemed to say. "Don't worry. Just trust, pray, and wait." Every time I was tempted to be anxious, I would sense the same message: "Wait on me. Don't try to solve it yourself. Just wait." I began again to rest in the Lord.

Every time I was tempted to be anxious, I would sense the same message: "Wait on me. Don't try to solve it yourself. Just wait." I began again to rest in the Lord.

WONDERFUL SURPRISES

After nine days, we flew back to New York City on a ten-hour overnight flight from Buenos Aires. I rested a few hours at home, then went to the church. My desk was piled high with mail, faxes, and phone messages. I started working through the pile about noon, and by late afternoon things really got interesting.

I opened two letters within the space of ten minutes that made my heart leap for joy. One was from a man in the Midwest with whom I had shaken hands once or twice. I wouldn't have recognized him that day if he had walked into my office. Yet his note said that God had impressed him to give us one million dollars for the new campus project. The second letter was from a group of people whom I had never met. They informed me that they would give us five million dollars!

Both gifts were unsolicited. The gifts totaled exactly six million dollars—the very amount with which I had struggled! The Lord obviously had not forgotten us while we were busy doing his work in South America. Nor had he forgotten the rest of the congregation praying at home.

God's "time of favor" had come; he helped us just as he had promised. We also learned another valuable lesson: when God's people believe and pray, the Lord *will* provide, but we must learn to wait on him with faithful, obedient hearts until the answer comes. This was a much-needed lesson since we still have many financial challenges ahead of us as we press on to complete the project.

Which lesson of faith is God seeking to teach you or the church you serve? Are you willing to trust him with the problems and heartaches you are facing today? Remember, he has not—*he cannot*—forsake or forget you, no matter how hopeless things may seem. He is waiting for you to transfer your problems . . . doubts . . . pain . . . and challenges into his hand in total trust.

Don't forget—he works for those who wait!

As you rest in the Lord, you can be sure that "the Lord longs to be gracious to you; he rises to show you compassion. For the Lord is a God of justice. Blessed are *all who wait for him!*" (Isaiah 30:18).

Heavenly Father, we praise you for all the grace and mercy you have shown us in the past. Teach us to pray more and trust in you with all our hearts. Give us the kind of faith that will wait patiently for the fulfillment of your promises. Help us to humble ourselves before you and listen carefully to your Word. Make us a holy and compassionate people so that others can see Jesus in our lives. We want our hearts to be your special home. In Christ's name, amen.

FRESH WIND, FRESH FIRE

*What Happens When
God's Spirit Invades the
Hearts of His People*

JIM CYMBALA
WITH DEAN MERRILL

In 1972, The Brooklyn Tabernacle's spark was almost out.
Then the Holy Spirit lit a fire
that couldn't be quenched.

Pastor Jim Cymbala shares the lessons
he learned when the Spirit ignited his heart and began to
move through his people. This unforgettable story will set a fire burn-
ing in your own heart to experience God's mercy, power, and love as
though for the first time.

> *"This is an important book for all those whose Christianity
> has become still and sterile. Fresh Wind, Fresh Fire sig-
> nals that God is at work in our day and that he wishes to be
> at work in our lives."*
>
> —DR. JOSEPH M. STOWELL

> *"This book will drive you to your knees. Be prepared to be
> provoked but also greatly challenged. You can be sure that
> reading this book will change you forever."*
>
> —DAVID WILKERSON

Hardcover 0-310-21188-3
Audio Pages® Abridged Cassettes 0-310-21199-9
Audio Pages® Unabridged CD 0-310-23649-5

Pick up a copy today at your favorite bookstore!

FRESH FAITH

What Happens When Real Faith Ignites God's People

JIM CYMBALA
WITH DEAN MERRILL

In an era laced with worry about the present and cynicism about the future, in a climate in which we've grown tired of hoping for miracles and wary of trumped-up claims that only disappoint, comes a confident reminder that God has not fallen asleep. He has not forgotten his people nor retreated into semi-retirement. On the contrary, he is ready to respond to real faith wherever he finds it.

Pastor Jim Cymbala insists that authentic, biblical faith is simple, honest, and utterly dependent upon God, a faith capable of transforming your life, your church, and the nation itself.

Jim Cymbala calls us back to the authentic, biblical faith—a fiery, passionate preoccupation with God that will restore our troubled children, our wounded marriages, and our broken and divided churches. Born out of the heart and soul of The Brooklyn Tabernacle, the message of *Fresh Faith* is illustrated by true stories of men and women whose lives have been changed through the power of faith.

Hardcover 0-310-23007-1
Audio Pages® Abridged Cassettes 0-310-23006-3
Audio Pages® Unabridged CD 0-310-23639-8

Pick up a copy today at your favorite bookstore!

FRESH POWER

Experiencing the Vast Resources of the Spirit of God

JIM CYMBALA
WITH DEAN MERRILL

Pastor Jim Cymbala of The Brooklyn Tabernacle has taught his congregation how God's mighty power can infuse their present-day lives and the mission of their church. He continued that teaching nationally in his best-selling books *Fresh Wind*, *Fresh Fire* and *Fresh Faith*, which tell about the transforming power of God's love to convert prostitutes, addicts, the homeless, and people of all races and stations in life.

Now in *Fresh Power* Cymbala continues to spread the word about the power of God's Holy Spirit in the lives of those who seek him. Fresh power, Cymbala says, is available to us as we desire the Holy Spirit's constant infilling and learn what it means to be Spirit filled, both as individuals and as the church. With the book of Acts as the basis for his study, Cymbala shows how the daily lives of first-century Christians were defined by their belief in God's Word, in the constant infilling of his Spirit, and in the clear and direct responses of obedience to Scripture. He shows that that same life in Christ through the power of the Holy Spirit is available today for pastors, leaders, and lay people who are longing for revival.

Hardcover 0-310-23008-X
Audio Pages® Abridged Cassettes 0-310-23467-X
Audio Pages® Unabridged CD 0-310-24200-2